D1436390

THE WORLD OF ADAM SMITH

THE WORLD OF
ADAM SMITH

BY
C. R. FAY, M.A., D.Sc.

(An expansion of lectures given at Toronto in the autumn of 1958)

CAMBRIDGE
W. HEFFER & SONS, LTD.

First published 1960

Printed in Great Britain at the Works of
W. HEFFER & SONS LTD., CAMBRIDGE, ENGLAND

CONTENTS

PREFACE

"Magna virum Mater! . . . The colonies owe to the policy of Europe the education and great views of their active and enterprising founders; and some of the greatest and most important of them, so far as concerns their internal government, owe to it scarce any thing else."—*Wealth of Nations*, II, 91.

Now, education is some thing; and thus fortified, light-blue Cambridge speaks to snow-white Canada from Belfast of orange hue.

This is a study of Adam Smith in relation to the economy of his age, as mirrored in *The Wealth of Nations*. It introduces at length two famous figures, Edmund Burke and F. M. Eden, together with the programme of a famous Chamber of Commerce—Glasgow—which was a stepping stone to the full Free Trade of nineteenth-century Britain. Adam Smith's closing years were spent in Edinburgh as a Commissioner of Customs for Scotland; and with him in mind we draw on the records of H.M. Customs and Excise in London and certain Outports, with their wealth of vivid detail, illustrating and enlarging what he has to say on timber, tobacco and coal, and their place in the pattern of an imperial economy. The Bicentenary of Robert Burns was celebrated in 1959; and though the two may never have met, they knew and admired one another's work. Burns' outburst of praise, after reading the *Wealth of Nations*, is familiar to readers of the Letters; and the last friendly service of the Edinburgh Commissioner of Customs was to recommend the Exciseman of Dumfries for a grant from the Salt Duty: incidentally, also, to bespeak four copies of the 1787 edition of the Poems.

Were the *Wealth of Nations* reviewed in 1960 for the first time, little surprise would be registered by potential readers (except in Marxian circles or the mien of patriot Scots), if the notices in the economic journals of the western world amounted, on the average, to 1½ pages—the full page a good-natured critique of the naivety, where not inadequacy, of the author's "tools of thought" (his economic theory, that is to say), and the half page a single paragraph commending Books III and IV to the attention of economic historians, with a concluding sentence of apology for the long ill-proportioned "unorganised" Book V, as the supererogation of old age. Well, opinion is free outside the Iron Curtain, and so, happily, is disagreement.

All references to the *Wealth of Nations* are to the two-volume edition by Edwin Cannan (Methuen).

CHAPTER I

EDMUND BURKE AND ADAM SMITH

Being a Lecture delivered at The Queen's University of Belfast,
April 27, 1956[1]

On the death of Thomas Wentworth, Earl of Strafford, that Lord
Deputy of Ireland who paid for his thoroughness with his head, his
rich Yorkshire estates passed by female descent to the 1st Marquis
of Rockingham. Rockingham is in Northants. On the death of
the 2nd Marquis (Burke's patron and friend), the estates passed,
again by female descent, to Earl Fitzwilliam, who later took the
name of Wentworth Fitzwilliam. He, too, was Burke's patron and
friend, and also his ardent disciple. This was that Earl Fitzwilliam
who in 1795, when it seemed that Pitt's ministry favoured Catholic
emancipation, was sent over as Lord Lieutenant of Ireland, but
went so far ahead of his instructions and was so intemperate in his
language towards his ministers that he had to be recalled after a
matter of weeks, to the sore disappointment of Burke. To him on
Burke's death the family entrusted his papers. The Earl's principal
seat was at Wentworth Woodhouse, which lies near Rotherham,
north of Sheffield. (It is now, of all things, the Physical Training
Centre of the West Riding County Council, its grounds scarred with
open-cast coal, and the Mausoleum to the 2nd Marquis with the
busts of Burke and other mourners in near-collapse.) Here the
Fitzwilliam family for a century and a half, in a great underground
safe, which one still may see, jealously guarded the Burke papers
and the equally valuable Strafford papers, until their recent transfer
to the Central Library, Sheffield, where one may now consult not
only the Wentworth Woodhouse muniments, but photostats of
Burke material in the possession of the Northants Record Society,
as also of individual letters in private ownership overseas—the
whole in readiness for the edition of the Burke Correspondence now
in progress under the direction of Professor T. W. Copeland, 3000
and more letters together with numerous fragments. Truly—for
after a month in the company of Burke a pun is almost incumbent—
"a feast of reading and a flow of scroll."

[1] Quotations from the Burke Correspondence by permission of Earl Fitzwilliam and his trustees.

In 1783 Michael Kearney, a Dublin friend writing to Burke, speaks of Belfast as "the Irish Boston." It would be indelicate of me to think of you as a body of incipient republicans. So by your leave I will change the metaphor and think of you as the Harvard of Northern Ireland. For just as Yale revels in Boswell, down to the lowest dreg, so Harvard with its Homer Vanderblue Collection of what it is pleased to call Smithiana has specialised in Adam Smith—all the editions of all his works in all the languages and all the books about him. Now between Scotland and Northern Ireland the contacts, as they relate to Adam Smith, are significant and several—Queen's, Armagh, Omagh, Edgeworthstown, this last not in Northern Ireland but not so far to the south.

You have by bequest in your Seminar Room at Queen's the classical portion of Smith's library with his bookplates in them. He was a "beau in his books," and like Burke reared on the classics; and to his first love he returned in his last years—his second love being strawberries, as grown in Scotland. *Pius Questus*, says Old Cato, *stabilissimusque, minimeque invidiosus; minimeque male cogitantes sunt, qui in eo studio occupati sunt.—W. of N.*, I, 427.[1]

Armagh—Adam Smith's revered teacher, the never-to-be-forgotten Francis Hutcheson, was a child of the manse. From Armagh he went to Dublin for his further education in the liberal Dublin of that day and then to Glasgow, to launch an academical revolution by lecturing in the mother tongue, interspersed with homely Doric, in place of the scholastic Latin in which in all the Universities of Britain lectures hitherto had been given. This was a factor in the liberalisation of the Scottish clergy; and to the high standard of pulpit eloquence thus evoked, Burke, the Irishman, of the Episcopal Church of England, in his turn contributed. For the Rev. John Erskine (the son of Adam Smith's Edinburgh colleague in his early days there) writes to Burke in 1779:

> The speeches the world has of yours have been and shall continue to be my only school for public speaking. I have repeated them daily aloud and have endeavoured (tho' Heaven knows with faint success) to catch at that animation and splendor of diction which give argument a projectile force impossible to be described but which all men feel who hear or read Mr. Burke.

And Hugh Blair, Blair of the Sermons (incidentally the friend who persuaded Adam Smith to compile an index to the *Wealth of Nations*

---

[1] "The (rural) Profession is honorable, most staunch, least grudging, and least do they harbour evil thoughts who are engaged in that pursuit."

which enhances for us the value of that work), writes to Burke in terms equally strong.

Omagh—the home of my great friend, the late Professor W. R. Scott, author of *Adam Smith as Student and Professor*, who discovered the treasures of Dalkeith—the early draft of the *Wealth of Nations* and the Townshend Papers. For Dalkeith, south of Edinburgh, was the seat of the young Duke of Buccleuch, with whom Adam Smith had travelled in France, 1764–66, and Charles Townshend, "Taxation Townshend," was his guardian.

Edgeworthstown—Sir Walter Scott, as a boy, knew Adam Smith and his circle. Several of the best stories, somewhat embroidered to be sure, come through him. In his Introduction to *The Betrothed* he refers playfully to the doctrine of "the immortal Adam Smith, concerning the division of labour"—the standard tag. And in the General Preface to *Waverley* he pays his famous tribute to Maria Edgeworth, saying that her studies of Irish character had turned him from poetry to prose, to become the "great unknown" of the Waverley novels, and that she had "done more towards completing the Union than perhaps all the legislative enactments by which it has been followed up."

This Union, for which Adam Smith had pleaded towards the end of the *Wealth of Nations*, II, 430 was desired (with reservations) by Burke, who in 1797 in almost the last letter from his pen wrote:

> My poor opinion is that the closest connection between Great Britain and Ireland is essential to the well being, I had almost said to the very being of the two Kingdoms. For that purpose I humbly conceive that the whole of the superior and what I would call imperial politics, ought to have its residence here [in England], and that Ireland locally, civilly and commercially independent, ought politically to look up to Great Britain in all matters of peace and war, and in a word with her to live and die.

The two principal actors on our stage were near co-evals—Adam Smith 1723–90, Edmund Burke 1729–97; and just as we cannot think of Smith without Hume, who died in 1776, a few months after the *Wealth of Nations* was published, so we cannot think of Burke without Oliver Goldsmith, one year his senior at Trinity College, Dublin—the statues of these her two greatest sons being today on either side of the Front Gate. In Sir Joshua Reynolds, the exact co-eval of Adam Smith, 1723–92, Smith and Burke had a common friend. To him Boswell in 1791 dedicated *The Life of Samuel Johnson, LL.D.*: and on his death in 1792 Burke wrote his epitaph.

Fond biographers have exalted the obligation of Adam Smith to their heroes. Hume anticipated him at every point; Burke was consulted by him; Franklin read his proof sheets; he got his theory from Turgot and the Physiocrats. It has been said and repeated, and it is all moonshine—apart from one story which is well supported and expresses truth, namely that in late life Adam Smith told Burke "after they had conversed on subjects of political economy, that he was the only man, who, without communication, thought on these topics exactly as he did."

Instead of inventing obligations, we should think rather of the pool of knowledge which each enriched and from which each drew; and in this connection pay special attention to the circle of their common friendships. Of these friends I will take four, all born in the early 1740's, and all of international repute—James Boswell the diarist, Arthur Young the agriculturist, William Eden (Lord Auckland) the diplomat, and Henry Dundas the statesman.

First, Boswell the brother Scot, who had studied under Smith at Glasgow. But he was no particular friend and in the Life rather gloats over the differences between Smith and Johnson. It was Professor John Anderson (of whom more anon) who supplied him with "Pray, Sir, have you seen Brentford?"—the Doctor's reply to Smith and his friends after they had shown him the sights of Glasgow: and it was at Anderson's house that Boswell tried to draw Johnson into trouncing the infidelities of Hume and Adam Smith. With Burke it is different. The references to him in the Life are apposite and friendly, though Burke's admirers would like more, and we have now in the Burke correspondence a fascinating run from Boswell to Burke. In it he is his shameless importunate self, begging for a letter or invitation to Gregories, and when he gets no reply, trying to draw him, for "I know you love a pun," by pronouncing his birth of Pallas allusion "a very *capital*" and asking for a return "in *kind*": reminding him how much they agreed on America: warning him that if the Popery bill were pressed it would bring a revolution, as indeed it almost did by bringing Lord George Gordon to London in the summer of 1780: and when Burke became Paymaster General, "your apotheosis, as poor Goldsmith said," begging for the office of Judge Advocate in Scotland or "some place of such an income as to enable me to keep house in London"; for in Edinburgh he said he felt "like a cat in an airpump." Surely this pestering Boswell was a fellow from whom Burke would be only too glad to escape; yet if one thinks so, one is very wrong, as a letter from Sir Joshua Reynolds to Bennet Langton, September 12, 1782, in the recently discovered "Portraits by Sir Joshua Reynolds" (published by Yale) conclusively proves.

> He [Boswell] writes in good spirits and expresses his longings after London. Mr. Burke often talks of him and appears to have great affection towards him. He says he is by much the most agreeable man he ever saw in all his life.

For Burke could talk, and Boswell could listen (and take it down): being in Johnson's word a very *clubbable* man. Significantly, this same letter mentions a conversation with Adam Smith on "why imitation pleases." Smith was writing on it. Reynolds had offered to supply him with his own written views on the topic, but Smith excused himself on the ground that his essay was already ripe for the printer.

Second, Young. No one who has read his Autobiography can forget the touching tribute he pays to Burke, after the last visit to his now failing friend in 1796—"the man who I hold to possess the greatest and most brilliant parts of any person of the age in which he lived, whose conversation has often fascinated me; whose eloquence has charmed; whose writings have delighted and instructed the world; and whose name will without question descend to the latest posterity."

This was the final retrospect on a friendship of 30 years: let us remark briefly on the successive stages. From his first tour in his own East Anglia, he goes north, and in the Northern Tour of 1770 Wentworth Woodhouse is the principal show place—the house magnificent, the views superb, its landlord (Burke was now his private secretary) a prince of improvers, "the whole husbandry of natural grass carried to its *ne plus ultra*." The Marquis overhears Young in confidential talk with a young lady and catches her words "amazingly fine turnips." "So, so, Mr. Young, you are getting farming confidences of Miss Danby." Next year, 1771, comes the Tour through the East and South of England, calling on Robert Bakewell at Dishley, "flesh before bone," and ending at Gregories, Beaconsfield, Bucks, the estate which Burke had bought in 1768 in part with a loan from Rockingham. Here Burke lived with his family—Mrs. Jane Burke, Richard his brother, Richard his son and the cousin so-called, Will Burke. Here he spent the happiest days of his tumultous mental life and here he farmed. "I stand in need of avocations of this kind to dissipate painful feelings, unpleasant reflexions and still more unpleasant prognostications"—he writes in a letter of August, 1791, to Fitzwilliam, when begging for a score of "large ewe sheep, particularly those with the longest tails" to be served by his Colchian ram—which Fitzwilliam duly sent.

In the Burke correspondence we find a run of letters for 1770–71, in which he tells Young all about his farming—folding of ewes, fattening of porkers, ploughing with oxen, drainage, manuring, deep ploughing—seed trials with turnips and cabbage and carrots— some of them just in time to get into Young's Tour, to the modest delight of their maker.

Then the Irish Tour of 1776–78, for which Burke supplied intro- ductions, as did Miss Danby's father, who secured for him the posi- tion of agent to Lord Kingsborough in Michelstown, Co. Cork, whence the Irish tour was launched.   From this classic I select just one topic—the statistical account of Waterford and Wexford and their flourishing provision trade, the volume of emigration thence to the American colonies and the earnings from the annual voyage of fishermen to Newfoundland, that trade which Burke had pronounced to be the most valuable trade we had in the world, because of its place in the criss-cross of ocean trade: fish and fish oils traded for Brazilian sugar and West Indian rum, and for the salt and wines of Portugal and the Mediterranean, the chief market for "merchantable" fish—all which, as Burke points out, made a negligible showing in the Tables of Imports and Exports.

And finally, and most famous of all, the *Travels in France* of 1787, 1788, 1789–90: the precursor and complement of Burke's *Reflexions* of November, 1790; 1789, praise for Rousseau "that splendid genius who made people love the country"; 1790, revolu- tion "absolutely necessary," "a real regeneration of the people to the privileges of human nature"; but followed in 1793 by *The Example of France*, in which he swings round to the position of Burke after the massacres of 1792 and the imprisonment of the Royal family.   Everyone remembers his comment on the sand dunes of Dunkirk, "The magic of *property* turns sand into gold."

I am not aware of any direct correspondence between Young and Smith, but the catalogue of Adam Smith's Library (James Bonar) shows that he had all Young's tours and other works down to 1776: and we know, too, that he was on terms of correspondence with Sir John Sinclair, who came to preside over the Board of Agri- culture of which Young was secretary.

Third, William Eden (Lord Auckland)—incidentally the uncle of Sir F. M. Eden, author of the *State of the Poor*, 1797, examined in detail in Chapter II. William Eden, the brilliant young lawyer of Eton and Christ Church, went to America with his chief Lord Carlisle on the abortive peace mission of 1778, then to Ireland as Chief Secretary, where he won golden opinions from all—Provost Hely-Hutchinson tells Burke they never had such a secretary. Before he leaves he helps to found the Bank of Ireland, and I noted in the Auckland papers a letter from Burke asking for a favour to a banking friend. Then comes the contact with Adam Smith. For when in 1779 North's ministry proposed Free Trade with Ireland and English commercial interests took alarm, Eden through Dundas procured from Adam Smith the well known letters declaring for free trade between England and Ireland in the interest of both countries, and similarly between the British Isles and the countries of Europe. In 1786 at the instance of Pitt he undertook the mission to Paris which resulted in the commercial treaty of 1786, which came into effect in June, 1787. Into the 3rd edition of the *Wealth of Nations*, 1784, Adam Smith introduced (Conclusion of the Mercantile System Book IV) new matter in favour of a treaty such as Eden was about to procure, with the help of the French physiocrats, headed by Dupont de Nemours. In August, 1791, when he was Ambassador at the Hague, Eden's is among the strongest of the congratulations to Burke on "your late admirable publication."

Fourth, Dundas, Henry Dundas, the young Lord Advocate, who brought the word STARVATION (*vide* O.E.D.) into the language through a maiden speech of 1775. Burke and the opposition said that the prohibition of trade with the colonies would lead to famine. Dundas *was afraid* that starving would not do it—and promptly was nicknamed Starvation Dundas. But he was in his way a liberal and never lost contact either with Burke or with Adam Smith (his Edinburgh seat, Melville Castle, lay next door to Dalkeith, which was Smith's second home). He secured the removal of disabilities inherited from the '45 and turned discontented clansmen into magnificent Highland regiments, officered by their hereditary leaders. He introduced the Catholic Relief Bill for Scotland, 1778; and instituted the probe into East Indian affairs, which Burke and Philip Francis pursued with such violence.[1] Upon the rise of Pitt, he brought the Scottish political machine to his support, and as head of the India Board, Home Secretary and Secretary for War and the Colonies, was Pitt's right hand man. At his London residence,

---

[1] I failed to find in the Burke correspondence any clue to the identity of Junius and, if he was Philip Francis, whether Burke was aware of it.

Wimbledon Manor, he and his chief counselled and caroused, lingering over the wine cup till their coach came to take them to Westminster.

> 'I cannot see the Speaker, Hal, can you?'
> 'Not see the Speaker! hang it, I see two.'

And it was at Wimbledon that the celebrated meeting of Smith and Pitt is said to have occurred. Adam Smith arriving late, the company rose to receive him. "Be seated, gentlemen," said Smith. "No," replied Pitt; "we will stand till you are seated, for we are all your scholars."

Dundas was Lord Rector of Glasgow in 1783: Burke in 1784 and 1785: a local landowner, Mr. Graham, in 1786: and Adam Smith, Glasgow's grand old man, in 1787. It is, therefore, not surprising to find such references to Adam Smith as these—

E.B. to Rockingham, April 27, 1782:

> Adam Smith, of whose sense and honesty I have a good opinion, has several times informed me and wished me to inform your Lordship that the Advocate [Dundas] . . . had great weight with the Duke of Buccleugh . . . and was capable of being firmly attached.

Dundas[1] to E.B., April 7, 1784:

> Adam Smith mentioned your wishes respecting Sir Gilbert Elliot [the son and heir of Adam Smith's contemporary and friend].

And so it all ties in. One might add that Wm. Eden married into the Gilbert Elliot family.

In addition to these great four of the early 1740's, Boswell, Young, Eden, Dundas, one must at least mention Charles James Fox, born in 1749. To expand this theme would require a lecture to itself. May I leave it to a cartoon—the dagger speech of December 28, 1792: the spectacled Burke, with daggers in either hand ready to cast them to the floor of the house, as from his mouth issues the legend "Plunderers, Assassins, Republicans," while in the rear, but still on the same side of the House, the burly form of Fox exclaims "Dam me, he's got the French disorders."

But now let us follow the literary and political career of Burke, and see where Adam Smith comes into it. In 1756 he earned in London his literary spurs with (1) *Vindication of Natural Society*, a subtle blend of irony and truth, and (2) *Essay on the Sublime and*

---

[1] Fox had replaced him as Advocate, August, 1783, by Henry Erskine, who declined "the abandoned habits" of his predecessor. If only E.B. had tabulated the best 50 puns he had perpetrated or been told! They would "tell well" surely.

Beautiful. About the former Young gives a pretty anecdote. A friend showing him Dodsley's Book of Authors' Receipts, said (pointing to *Vindication*, 6 guineas—Will Burke) "So much for kindling the revolution": and "now for putting it out" £1,000, signed E.B.

In the *Sublime and Beautiful* comes the only mention of Cambridge University that I know of—the case of Nicholas Saunderson, the professor of mathematics, who was able to lecture on light and colour, though blind from the age of one. He lived in my own College (Christ's), though he was not a fellow, and his portrait is now on the first floor landing of the University offices. The central theme of the *Essay* is this—

> Sympathy must be considered as a sort of substitution by which we are put into the place of another man and affected in many respects as he is affected.

It could well serve as a motto for Adam Smith's *Theory of Moral Sentiments*, 1759: surely the two would shortly come together, as indeed they did. I quote by permission from an unpublished letter from Burke to Smith, September 10, 1759, in the possession of Mr. J. M. Osborn, U.S.A.

> Sir,
>
> I am quite ashamed that the first letter I have the honour of writing to you should be an apology for my conduct. It ought to be entirely taken up with my thanks to you for the satisfaction I received from your very agreeable and instructive work, but I cannot do that pleasing act of justice without apologising at the same time for not having done it much earlier. When I received the Theory of Moral Sentiments from Mr. Hume, I ran through it with great eagerness; I was immediately after hurried out of town, and involved ever since in a variety of troublesome affairs. My resolution was to defer my acknowledgments until I had read your book with proper care and attention; to do otherwise with so well studied a piece would be to treat it with great injustice. It was indeed an attention extremely well bestowed and abundantly repaid. I am not only pleased with the ingenuity of your theory; I am convinced of its solidity and truth; and I do not know that it ever cost me less trouble to admit so many things to which I had been a stranger before. I have ever thought that the old systems of morality were too contracted and that this science could never stand upon any narrower basis than the whole of human nature. . . .
>
> A theory like yours founded on the nature of man, which is always the same, will last, when those that are founded on his opinions, which are always changing, will and must be forgotten. I own I am particularly pleased with those easy and happy illustrations from

common life and manners [the very point on which Burns seized in his eulogy of the *Wealth of Nations*] in which your work abounds more than any other that I know by far. . . .

Philosophers very frequently miss a thousand things that might be of infinite advantage. . . . It seems to require that infantine simplicity which despises nothing to make a good philosopher, as well as to make a good Christian. . . . My delay on this occasion may, I am afraid, make it improper for me to ask any favour from you. But there is one I have too much at heart not to sacrifice any propriety to attain it. It is, that whenever you come to town, I may have the honour of being made personally known to you. I shall take the liberty of putting this office on our friend Mr. Hume, who has already so much obliged me by giving me your book.

I am, Sir, with the truest esteem for your work and your character

Your most obliged and obedient servant,

EDMUND BURKE.

(An entertaining letter from Hume to Adam Smith explains the gift and foreshadows a crucial episode in Smith's life.

Lisle Street, Leicester Fields.

April 12, 1759.

Dear Smith,

I give you thanks for the agreeable Present of your Theory. . . . I sent one to . . . Burke, an Irish Gentleman, who wrote lately a very pretty Treatise on the Sublime. . . .

Charles Townsend, who passes for the cleverest Fellow in England is so taken with the performance, that he said to Oswald he wou'd put the Duke of Buccleugh under the Authors Care, and would endeavour to make it worth his while to accept of that Charge. . . ."

Henry Scott, the 3rd Duke of Buccleuch, 1746–1812, succeeded his grandfather the 2nd Duke in 1751, and Townshend the 2nd husband of his mother, the Countess of Dalkeith, became thus the boy's guardian. Adam Smith acted as his tutor for some 3 years, being with him in France from February, 1764, to October, 1766, and thereafter his lifelong friend.

See *New Letters of David Hume*, edited by Raymond Klibansky and Ernest C. Mossner, Oxford, 1954. Letter 29, pp. 51–55.)

The book was reviewed by Burke in the Annual Register for 1759, which he launched then and conducted for many years. Thus both Burke and Smith arrived at Political Economy through Moral Philosophy. But when and where did he learn the former? This he tells us in the *Letter to a Noble Lord* of 1796:

The first session I sat in Parliament [as member for Wendover, Bucks, 1766] I found it necessary to analyse the whole commercial, financial,

constitutional and foreign interests of Great Britain and its empire.
If I had not deemed it of some value, I should not have made political
economy an object of hy humble studies from my very early youth to
near the end of my service in Parliament, even before (at least to any
knowledge of mine) it had employed the thoughts of speculative men
in other parts of Europe. At that time it was still in its infancy in
England, where in the last century it had its origin. Great and
learned men thought my studies not wholly thrown away, and
deigned to communicate with me now and then some particulars of
their immortal works.

I think that here he had in mind Young and Smith, and perhaps
also Hume and Franklin. "My very early youth"—most true,
for in No. 7 of the Reformer, 1748, that remarkable undergraduate
magazine, written mainly by the precocious young scholar who
haunted Trinity College library, we read

That some should live in a more sumptuous manner than others, is
very allowable, but sure it is hard that those who cultivate the soil
should have so small a part of its fruits, and that among creatures of
the same kind there should be such a disproportion in their manner of
living. It is a kind of blasphemy on Providence.

In 1774–80, as member for Bristol, he reached the height of his
Parliamentary oratory with the Speeches on American Taxation,
April, 1774, and Conciliation with America, March, 1775. From
the former I allow myself this quotation:—

Leave America, if she has taxable matter in her, to tax herself. . . .
Leave the Americans as they anciently stood, and these distinctions,
born of our unhappy contest, will die along with it. . . . Be content
to bind America by laws of trade; you have always done it. Let this
be your reason for binding their trade. Do not burthen them with
taxes; you were not used to do so from the beginning. Let this be
your reason for not taxing. (Cf. 'Magnanimity in politics is not
seldom the truest wisdom; and a great empire and little minds go ill
together.')

Of the speech on Conciliation there is a full synopsis in Burke's hand
in the Burke papers. Reading it, one acclaims it as nothing less
than the Charter of the Second Empire. But now, remembering
that Adam Smith in the winter of 1766–67 fed Charles Townshend
with the material for his luckless budget of 1767, let us read the last
lines of the *Wealth of Nations*, which was nearing completion, even
as Burke spoke.

If the project [of empire] cannot be completed, it ought to be given
up. If any of the provinces of the British empire cannot be made to
contribute to the support of the whole empire, it is surely time that

Great Britain should free herself from the expence of defending those provinces in time of war, and of supporting any part of their civil or military establishments in time of peace, and endeavour to accommodate her future views and designs to the real mediocrity of her circumstances.

"Real mediocrity"—unthinkable.   But which of the two was right, Burke or Smith?   I fear I must say Burke, in the company of the old cynic he had long admired, whose motto was "let sleeping dogs lie."

As member for Bristol, Burke rendered many services to his constituents, notably to John Noble, of the firm of Noble and Pinson (Bristol and Dartmouth), pioneers of the fishery on the Labrador, and to Richard Champion, the porcelain manufacturer, which is the occasion of the second letter to Adam Smith, May 1, 1775, asking him to facilitate the passage of Champion's private bill through the Lords with the assistance of the Duke of Buccleuch.   It duly became law by 15 Geo. 3, c. 52, despite the opposition of Wedgwood and the Staffordshire potters.   But upon the proposals for free trade with Ireland, which Burke supported, there came a rift in the lute.   A Quaker supporter (and they were powerful in Bristol) wrote to him "We do not find one among us who can declare in favour of thy sentiments."   His friends hoped that he would continue to represent them, but soft pedalling his Irish views, to which he replied in terms that have become classic.

Burke to Noble, April 24, 1778.

> I do not wish to represent Bristol or to represent any place, but on terms that shall be honourable to the chosen and the choosers.   I do not desire to sit in Parliament for any other end than that of promoting the common happiness of all those who are in any degree subjected to our legislative authority and of binding together in one common tie of civil interest and constitutional freedom every denomination of men among us.

After 1780 he sat for Malton, in N.E. Yorks, the family constituency of Rockingham and Fitzwilliam.

Preoccupation with politics did not encroach on his literary friendships, for he, like Goldsmith, was an original member of the Literary Club founded by Reynolds in 1764, where the range of talk was wide, and politics as welcome as theology or letters.   Adam Smith and Thomas Barnard, Dean of Derry (later Bishop of Limerick), were elected in December, 1775, next in the list to Gibbon.   The egregious Boswell writes to his friend Temple, April, 1776, "Smith too is one of our club.   It has lost its select merit!!"   The

Dean of Derry it was, who, on Goldsmith's death in 1774, organised the round robin (facsimile in Boswell), which was licked into shape by Burke, asking that the epitaph on the monument which the Club was to erect in Westminster Abbey might be in English: which drew from Dr. Johnson: "Tell 'Mund Burke I should have thought he had more sense"—he (J.) "would never disgrace the walls of Westminster Abbey with an inscription in English." In punishment, perhaps, for the round robin, the Doctor fell on its originator at Sir Joshua's dinner table. The Dean had remarked that after 45 a man did not improve. J.: "I differ from you, Sir; a man may improve, and you yourself have great room for improvement." The Dean was taken aback for they were good friends before (and after) the incident, and next morning he sent to Sir Joshua a poem, from which I take the last two stanzas:

> If I have thoughts and can't express 'em
> Gibbon shall teach me how to dress 'em
> In terms select and terse,
> Jones teach me modesty—and Greek,
> Smith how to think, Burke how to speak
> And Beauclerk to converse.

> Let Johnson teach me how to place
> In fairest light each borrow'd grace;
> From him I'll learn to write
> Copy his clear and easy style
> And from the roughness of his file
> Grow as himself—polite.

Sir William Jones was the oriental scholar; Topham Beauclerk, the young Oxonian, grandson of a Duke, who once took the Doctor for a "frisk" with the girls in Covent Garden. The poem is given in full in a letter of January 5, 1776, from R. Burke, Sr., to Will Burke.

1776 and 1777 are the years when from the records of the Club attendances Burke and Gibbon must most frequently have met. By 1778 Adam Smith had gone North in order to take up the duties of Customs Commissioner in Edinburgh—secured for him at the instance of Dundas—and so missed the celebrated debate at the Club between Burke and Johnson on emigration. Did emigration cause depopulation?

E. "Leave a few breeders, and you'll have more people than if there were no emigration."

J. "Nay, Sir, it is plain there will be more people if there are more breeders. Thirty cows in good pasture will produce more calves than ten cows, provided they have good bulls."

E. There are bulls enough in Ireland. . . ."

1780 was a big year for Burke in Parliament. For on February 11, 1780, he presented to the House his Plan for Economical Reform —the abolition of sinecures and of useless, but costly offices, and stricter accounting in public finance.

> In proportion as I am tender of the past [for he would not disturb existing holders] I will be provident of the future. All money that was formerly imprested to the two great pay-offices, I would have imprested in future to the Bank of England. These offices should, in future, receive no more than cash sufficient for small amounts. Their other payments ought to be made by drafts on the bank, expressing the service. A cheque account, from both offices, of drafts and receipts, should be annually made up in the exchequer: charging the bank in the account with the cash balances, but not demanding the payment until there is an order from the treasury, in consequence of a vote in parliament.

This was done in due course both for the Army and the Navy, and for the latter was the subject of special legislation in 1785, 25 Geo. 3 c. 31 (Treasurer of the Navy). Burke, as Paymaster for the Army in 1782 and 1783, suffered financially by the change, and Dundas's subsequent irregularities under the Act of 1785 figured among the charges for which, as Lord Melville, he was impeached in 1805. In the latter year Huskisson (who had begun his public life under Dundas and was now at the Treasury) completed the reform by applying the same rule to the receipts of the Receiver General.

But two other proposals were less well conceived: one was for the abolition of the Board of Trade, which, as reorganised by Lord Hawkesbury and expanded by Huskisson in his great Presidency of 1823-27, was of essential value in the introduction of free trade and the moulding of the New Empire by a policy of imperial preference. Equally shortsighted was his proposal (though here he had the authority of the *Wealth of Nations* behind him—II, 309) for the sale of Crown Lands, the revenue from which was then negligible. In my chapter on Woods, Forests and Crown Lands (*Huskisson and his Age*, Ch. 7) I have tried to show how Huskisson, as First Commissioner, 1814-23, salvaged the Crown Estate and set it on the road to becoming a great public asset, especially in respect of its rich London estate, as profitable as, and more enduring than, Disraeli's famous investment in the Shares of the Suez Canal.

And so Huskisson, too, links with Burke and Adam Smith.

It was also a big year for London; when in the first days of June the "metropolitan seat of Empire" was at the mercy of Lord George Gordon and the mob.

"What's that?" said Lord George. . . . "A devil, a kettle, a Grip, a Polly, a Protestant, no Popery" cried the raven. . . . The rioters pelt our people. Our people retire before the rioters. Stones are thrown, insults are offered, not a shot's fired. Why? Because of the magistrates. Damn the magistrates!"—*Barnaby Rudge*, Chs. 57, 58.

Burke describes his part in it in a letter on June 13 to John Noble. After lodging his wife and books in safety, he kept guard in the streets for four nights, walked among the crowd "and even found friends and well-wishers among the blue cockades," passed fearlessly and quite unharmed through the crowd to the House. It was (he said) perhaps as well they heard the "flagitious petition": otherwise "the subsequent ravages would have been charged on our obstinacy." And he concludes:

> There is much to be done to repair the ruins of our country and its reputation, as well as to console the number of families ruined by wickedness masking itself under the cloud of religious zeal.

Adam Smith was a sluggish correspondent, and 1782–83 yield the only three letters to Burke—brief notes in the familiar schoolboy fist—a condolence of July 1, 1782, on the death of Rockingham, and of July 6 on Burke's consequent departure from office—"Tout est perdu horsmis l'honneur . . .; and when honour is not only perfectly and completely saved, but acquired and augmented, all other losses are insignificant. . . . Farewell, my dear friend, I hope we shall soon meet again even in this world in times of more joy and prosperity"; and April 15, 1783, a congratulation on his return to office—"Be so good as to remember me in the most respectful and most affectionate manner to Mrs. Burke and to your brother"—Custom House, Edinburgh. To this last Burke replies from the Horse Guards, June 20, 1783, "That such a friend, and such a man as you are, should take any concern in my fortunes is a circumstance very flattering to me. . . . All is settled again; and in great apparent tranquillity on the old foundations. But we walk the streets of Naples." Burke spoke truly, for when the Lords threw out Fox's India bill, the uneasy coalition of Fox and North came to an end and Pitt's long reign began. But just before he received from His Majesty the curt notice of dismissal from office (December 19, 1783), he had accepted the office of Lord Rector of Glasgow. Principal Leechman (December 5), in returning the University's thanks for the honour he had done them in consenting to serve as "Chief Magistrate of the University," asks him to keep in touch with the trustees of the recent Hunter bequest of his Museum and Library [William Hunter, 1718–83] and to allow the University "as with all your predecessors in office to write letters and to send papers to our solicitor [in Lincoln's Inn] under your cover"!

Hence it is that we have for 1784 and 1785 a run of 11 long letters from the Principal and his chief lieutenant, John Millar, relating to University business (but unhappily none of Burke's replies), and from other sources details of his two visits to Scotland, in which Adam Smith figures as travelling companion and host.

April, 1784, he goes to Edinburgh in the company of Lord Maitland (James Maitland, Earl of Lauderdale, author of the "Thoughts on the Circulation in Ireland, 1805," which doctrinally is a half-way house to the Bullion Committee's Report of 1810) to be welcomed by friends, old and new, Adam Smith, Principal Robertson, Sir William Forbes the banker of Pitsligo, and Sir John Dalrymple, who sends a regular guide book of instructions—that worthy baronet of Cranston, to whom Johnson and Boswell were deliberately rude by arriving late for the dinner party in their honour. A halt at Hatton, Maitland's place, and then (it is now Good Friday) on to Glasgow, attended by Andrew Dalzel, the historian of Edinburgh University, Dugald Stewart, Smith's first biographer, and Adam Smith himself. At Glasgow their host is John Millar, Maitland's old tutor: and on Saturday, April 10, the Installation.

Annual Register. Chronicle of Events, April 10, 1784:—

> The Rt. Hon. Edmund Burke was installed in the office of lord rector of the University of Glasgow, he was attended by several persons of rank and eminence; the spectators were very numerous and testified their satisfaction by the highest marks of approbation and applause. His lordship, after taking the oaths of office, addressed the meeting in a polite and eloquent speech suited to the occasion. Having attended public worship in the college chapel, he was afterwards entertained by the gentlemen of the University.

On the 11th he and Maitland and Adam Smith made an excursion to Loch Lomond, where Professor Rouet received them, and returned to Edinburgh via Carron, where they saw the iron works. Then the Lord Rector goes back to London, with honours following shortly— Fellowship of the Royal Society of Edinburgh, July 20, on the part of Professor Dalzel; Freedom of the City of Glasgow on the part of Patrick Colquhoun, Chairman of the newly founded Glasgow Chamber of Commerce.

After Burke's time there arose a legend, which is totally un-
supported by contemporary evidence, that he "faltered" and
concluded his speech abruptly by saying that "he had never before
addressed so learned an audience." My guess is that his audience
expected fireworks and that he spoke quietly and briefly, quite
possibly observing by way of compliment that he felt shy in the
presence of such a gathering. Yet if they had followed him to
Westminster in the columns of the *Glasgow Mercury*, they would
have seen, if not fireworks, at least illumination. For when Pitt
in his Budget proposed a tax on candles, Burke rose "in order to
throw some light on the subject," and to that end desired the clerk
to read the proceedings respecting the recall of Elijah Impey and
Warren Hastings! Mr. Burke, says the reporter, "then dwelt on
his favourite topic of condemning"; and after Pitt had replied, "the
Speaker, apprehending that the duty on candles had been sufficiently
illustrated by the pertinent observations of the Honourable Gentleman, whose fancy sometimes carried him beyond the Ganges and the
Persian Gulf and led him by a retrograde motion to Leadenhall
Street and St. Stephen's Chapel, put the question relating to the
duty on candles, which was carried without opposition, but not
without considerable laughter from all quarters of the House."

One is reminded of the famous exchange between George Grenville
and the Great Commoner: "Tell me where I can lay another tax—
Gentle shepherd tell me where";[1] wherat the House was so convulsed
with laughter that business was for a time suspended.

But politicians must have their holiday, and September sees them
in the fields, not to shoot game, but in Moorfields to watch the ascent
of M. Lunardi in his balloon—the Prince of Wales, Mr. Fox,[2] Mr.

---

[1] From Solomon A Serenata, 1742. Air:—
                Tell me, lovely Shepherd, where
                . . . . etc.
            Gentle Shepherd, tell me where?

[2] In *Table Talk*, p. 85, Samuel Rogers tells what befell C. J. F. that day.

"I saw Lunardi make the first ascent in a balloon which had been witnessed
in England. It was upon the Artillery Ground. Fox was there with his
brother General F. The crowd was immense. Fox happening to put his
hand down to his watch, found another hand upon it, which he immediately
seized. "My friend," said he to the owner of the strange hand, "you have
chosen an occupation which will be your ruin at last." "O, Mr. Fox" was the
reply, "forgive me and let me go! I have been driven to this course by
necessity alone; my wife and children are starving at home." Mr. Fox, always
tender-hearted, slipped a guinea into the hand, and then released it.

On the conclusion of the show, Fox was proceeding to look what o'clock it
was. "Good God," cried he, "my watch is gone!!"—"Yes," answered General
F, "I know it is; I saw your friend take it." "Saw him take it! and you made
no attempt to stop him?"—"Really, you and he appeared to be on such good
terms with each other that I did not choose to interfere."

Sheridan, Mr. Burke, Lord North and many others. "Not a plain
or eminence, a window or a roof, a chimney or a steeple, within the
sight of Bedlam, but what were previously thronged." But Ireland
was first in the field on April 18 with a similar display by M. Rosseau
at Navan, Co. Meath. Only there the Castle made a political issue
of it; for a drummer was slipped into the basket, and after the
balloon had vanished into the clouds, the assembled thousands
heard for full fifteen minutes the rousing notes of the "British
Grenadiers."

1785. A second term of office, and a second visit to Glasgow for
the ceremony on September 1. At Edinburgh he, with his son and
William Windham, was the guest of Sir Gilbert Elliot (Lord Minto
to be): and in Windham's published diary we can follow their
course. They dined with Adam Smith on the outward and return
journey not once, but several times, and Thomas Somerville in
My own Life and Times, 1741–1814, tells of an evening party where
Burke was at the top of his form. "All sorts of subjects, politics,
criticism, theology were introduced and I was astonished at the
brilliance of his language and the universality of his knowledge."
At Glasgow no speech: Windham's diary reading: "September 1,
Ceremony of Burke's Admission. None but boys present. . . .
Dined in the college hall; present Dr. Stevenson, Mr. Millar, Lord
Maitland and Burke. . . . I was soon obliged to go away to attend
the Committee of Operative Weavers who were assembled in our
inn in honour of Lord Maitland and Burke. [There was apparently
some thought of adopting Windham as a candidate for Parliament.
He was then a Whig, later Pitt's secretary at war, and known as
'Weathercock Windham.'] From the inn we were conducted in
grand and orderly procession; the windows on each side being lined,
and a transparency with different superscriptions carried before us,
to Dr. Stevenson's, where we were to sup."

A tour of Inverary and the Western Highlands followed, as we
learn from Burke's letter of thanks to the Duchess of Argyle. On
the way back to London they called at Wentworth Woodhouse.

But the strangest part of the story remains to be told. For
during most of his period of office, at the urgent solicitation of
Leechman and Millar, he was hard at work trying to counteract the
subversive activities of the notorious Professor Anderson. In
January, 1785, and after, the Professor was trying to procure a
Royal Visitation to enquire into alleged abuses, caballing at taverns
with the malcontents, securing signatures to his petition from "a

multitude of boys in the Humanity Class of 11, 12, and 13 years of age," consorting with "the lowest of the Scotch and Irish students" and kindling anew the embers of religious intolerance among the "Fanatical Party." "The Principal," writes Millar, November 13. "I am afraid will drop very soon," and in fact he died before the end of the year.

Burke in London, with the aid of the Lord Advocate, Sir Ilay Campbell, defeated the petition: and Millar in a postscript to his final letter of November 13 is able to say:

> I have the pleasure of informing you that our colleges instead of suffering by the late attempts, have the appearance of being fuller this season than they have ever been for some years.

But one suspects that these feuds of long standing (for Anderson was causing trouble even in Smith's day—Professor Macfie discovered only a month ago in the University Archives a letter of Adam Smith's, notifying a year's leave of absence for the trouble maker in 1756), in conjunction with the loss of Smith, Black and Cullen, were a factor in the transfer of academic primacy to Edinburgh.

There remain two letters of Burke to Adam Smith, of December 7 and December 20, 1786, in which he asks Smith to use his influence on behalf of Will Burke, who was now in India. Adam Smith (the letter is in Scott, *Adam Smith as Student and Professor*, p. 300) duly writes to Col. Ross, singing the praises of "my old and most valuable friend, Mr. William Burke" in the terms indicated by Edmund. And Scott in a footnote appends Lord Cornwallis's reply of December 2, 1789[1]:

> I have ever since I have been in India treated William Burke with the greatest possible attention and I have done some little favours. . . . But it is impossible for me to serve him essentially, that is, to put large sums of money in his pocket, without gross violation of my public duty and doing acts for which I should deserve to be impeached.

Will Burke was not the only one of Edmund's friends whose financial operations were open to question.

Adam Smith died on July 17, 1790; and the last seven years of Burke's life are therefore outside our province, with the exception of one year, 1795. The loss of his only son Richard on August 2, 1794, all but broke him, but he rallied grandly for a final fight.

---

[1] The very month, December 18, 1789, in which Adam Smith had the easier task of commending to Joseph Banks "Mr. Leslie, a young gentleman of great merit"—Sir John Leslie to be, Edinburgh's Professor of Natural Philosophy.

The *Thoughts on Scarcity*, 1795, in the shape of a memorandum to Pitt, published posthumously, clinches the doctrinal affinity with Adam Smith. Because more downright, it was more serviceable even than the *Wealth of Nations* to Cobden and the Anti Corn Law League in their fight for free food. Agriculture (the argument runs) is a trade and must be conducted on the principle of trade: no stoppage of the distilleries (there is a delicious passage in Praise of Gin); no renewal of the statutes against engrossing and forestalling—the last remnant of which he had himself removed from the statute book; no government granaries—"The best, and indeed the only good granary is the rickyard of the farmer. This and the barn enjoying many of the same advantages have been the sole granaries of England from the foundation of its agriculture to the present."

Thus the landlord-farmer, who at the moment of writing was straining every nerve to get the last ounce of food-stuff from his land, and in addition raising cavalry horses to resist a French invasion. But of all the links that we have observed none is more remarkable than the link at this point with, of all persons, his arch enemy Warren Hastings. For, as I have noted in *Huskisson and his Age*, p. 282, Hastings wrote two memoranda in the scarcity years of 1795 and 1800, with his very different solutions based on his famine experience in India—solutions which foreshadow the policy of Indian Famine Relief in the late nineteenth century and the measures taken by our own Ministry of Food in World War II. Truly in economics, as in politics and morals, the conflict is not always between right and wrong, but sometimes rather between right and right.

And here we must take our leave of Adam Smith and Edmund Burke, friends and fellow thinkers over the years, drawing from, as well as contributing to, the circle in which they moved, the one the father of our political economy, the other the noblest figure in the long roll of our political philosophy. To these two, the Scotsman and the Irishman, the debt of England is immeasurably great.

CHAPTER II

TWO LITERARY DISCIPLES OF THE EIGHTEENTH CENTURY

SAMUEL CRUMPE AND F. M. EDEN

Interpolations inside quotations are in square brackets.

Where authors are concerned, the test of true discipleship is intelligent assimilation of the master. Crumpe and Eden, the two writers here under review, pass the test triumphantly. Yet neither took any special interest in money or trade as such. The *Wealth of Nations* was to them a bible which unfolded the laws of society. It was "political," in the ample sense of "social," economy.

The first of the two writers, Samuel Crumpe (1766–96), was a Limerick doctor, M.D. of Dublin, who died at the early age of 29. In 1793 he published a prize essay (pp. 365) inscribed to James Earl of Charlemont, President of the Royal Irish Academy, with the title

ESSAY ON THE BEST MEANS OF PROVIDING EMPLOYMENT FOR THE PEOPLE.

He has the *Wealth of Nations* at his side throughout and quotes accurately, with page references, which for convenience I have turned into those of Cannan's edition. (As later the quotations in Eden.)

PART I. GENERAL.

Necessaries and Luxuries.

20 "The nature of each is very well defined by that celebrated writer Dr. A. Smith, whose treatise, on the Wealth of Nations, is an invaluable fund of political knowledge and whose sentiments we shall have frequent occasion to recur to in the present essay." Quoting the lines on II, 354–5 from "By necessaries" down to "lowest rank of the people," he concludes "Such comforts and conveniences as Dr. Smith describes may, I think, be termed the *artificial necessaries* of life; the articles of mere subsistence may be called absolute or natural necessaries."

23 "The woolen coat is, as Smith observes, the produce of the joint labours of a multitude of workmen. The shepherd . . . all join their different arts in order to produce them"—as on I, 13, with abbreviations.

33 "'In mercantile and manufacturing towns, says Smith [I, 318], where the inferior ranks of people are chiefly maintained by the employment of capital, they are in general industrious, sober, and thriving; as in many English, and in most Dutch towns. In those towns which are principally supported by the constant, or occasional residence of a court, and in which the inferior ranks of people are chiefly maintained by the spending of revenue, they are in general idle, dissolute, and poor; as at Rome, Versailles, Compiegne, and Fontainbleau.' To the list we may surely add Dublin."

Arthur O'Connor, the Protestant rebel, who served under Bonaparte and married Mlle. Condorcet, had the same thought, but used it for the discomfiture of Adam Smith and Co. "If you wish to be informed of Irish politics and Irish finances, it is not by reading Harrington nor Sydney nor Locke nor Stewart nor Montesquieu nor Smith's Wealth of Nations. No! it is the Court Calendar you must examine. . . ."—*State of Ireland* (1798), 2nd ed., 33. It reminds one of the fate of "Nation of Shopkeepers." Introduced in the *Wealth of Nations*, it has come to be ascribed to Napoleon, alike in England and France.

Wages.

41 "The wages of labour, as Smith observes [I, 83], are the encouragement of industry, which, like every other human quality, improves in proportion to the encouragement it receives." (This in *Wealth of Nations* comes after a paragraph which says that the progressive state is best for the labouring poor.) And following Smith's argument he continues:

42 "The liberal reward of labour, besides its immediate effect in increasing the industry and exertions of the individual, has a similar tendency indirectly by the encouragement it gives to population."

44 "Doctor Smith could not find upon examination that the variation of the produce of the linen manufacture in Scotland or of the woollen manufacture in Yorkshire bore any sensible connection with the dearness or cheapness of the seasons"—adverting to I, 86.

45 "If liberal wages ever do discourage industry it must be . . . because the increase is sudden and transitory. A settled liberal reward of labour can never produce such an effect."

Thus Crumpe, like his master, was of the elect few, a believer in high wages. In Smith's matchless phrasing, "The liberal reward of labour, therefore, as it is the effect of increasing wealth, so it is the cause of increasing population. To complain of it, is to lament over

the necessary effect and cause of the greatest public prosperity."
(I, 83.)   But the doctrine was repulsive to the prudence of the well-
to-do; and after 1798 the liberalism of 1776 stood little chance
against the cottage-levelling parson of Jesus College, Cambridge,
with pestilence in one pocket and famine in the other.   From 1798
to 1834 the social influence of Adam Smith cannot compare with
that of Malthus.

49   "The employment of capital, therefore, in any country is a
      principal encouragement to the industry of its inhabitants.
      The celebrated Doctor Smith deems it its chief source and
      support"—paraphrasing I, 318-9.   "The proportion, says he,
      between capital and revenue" down to "real wealth and revenue
      of all its inhabitants."   (I, 319-20.)

This last a long and exact quotation.   Crumpe, it becomes clear,
was interested in the theory of the matter.

In Section II of Part I, *Impediments to Industry*, he is thinking
of the tax incidence analysis of *Wealth of Nations*, Book V; and, as
there (II, 404-5), so here poor old France gets it in the neck[1]:

74   "Hear the opinion of the eloquent Raynal on the effects of such
      injudicious imposts—the epithet echoing Smith's 'according to
      the eloquent and, sometimes, well informed Author of the
      Philosophical and Political History of the Establishment of
      the Europeans in the two Indies.'"   (I, 208.)

91   "In England, the principal manufacturing towns are exempt from
      Corporation restrictions: as instance, we may cite Manchester,
      Leeds, Birmingham and a considerable portion of London, viz.
      Westminster, Southwark, and the suburbs." (Cf. I, 122.[2])

Section III.   The System of Commerce and the System of Agriculture
      "I shall have frequent recourse to that invaluable political
      performance, the Inquiry of Dr. Smith" and "shall frequently
      the liberty of copying his words, distinguishing them only by
      inverted commas."

110   "What is prudence in the conduct of a private family can
      scarcely be folly in a great kingdom" (nearly as on I, 422);
      and then (unlike Charles Fox, who used the analogy to make a

---

[1] But the reproach was not always of English provenance.   In 1759, after
the military failures in Canada, a patriot saluted her with
              O France la sexe femelle
                Est toujours ton destin
            Ton bonheur vient d'une pucelle
            Ton malheur vient d'une catin
                  (to wit, the Pompadour).

[2] See below, p. 34, for Eden on the same subject.

different point—a nation like an individual must live within its means) Crumpe gives us Adam Smith's own point—if a foreign country can supply us with a commodity cheaper than we ourselves can make it, better buy it of them with some part of the produce of our own industry, employed in a way in which we have some advantage.

Crumpe's text now becomes an abstract of *Wealth of Nations*, Book IV, with long quotations from Bk. IV, Ch. II, on Restraints on Particular Imports and the Balance of Trade absurdity:

123   "Those who wish for more particular information on such subjects we have only again to refer to Doctor Smith's inestimable treatise on The Wealth of Nations."

134   The System of Agriculture—"author Quesnay *vide* Smith." Also, says Crumpe, consult "New and Old Principles of Trade compared; or a Treatise on the Principles of Commerce between Nations—published by Johnson, London, 1789, 8vo."

Part II.   Ireland.

There is much from Arthur Young, whose Tour in Ireland was now a classic; and Adam Smith gets a mention on potatoes as a culture. Crumpe's reference is to *Wealth of Nations*, I, 160–2.   But here the master's prescience had failed him.   "It is difficult," says Adam Smith,

"to preserve potatoes through the year, and impossible to store them like corn, for two or three years together.   The fear of not being able to sell them before they rot, discourages their cultivation, and is, perhaps, the chief obstacle to their ever becoming in any great country, like bread, the principal vegetable food of all the different ranks of the people." (I, 162.)

But if population is any criterion of greatness, Ireland by 1793 was heading that way, just because she had found in the potato another, if precarious, staff of life.

Crumpe is now in his own country; and he writes against a background of poverty and legal oppression, with gentlemen bullies here and combination-prone workmen there.   But the nicest bit of local colour, all the nicer for being meant as reproach, is

184   "Nothing is more common than to see a weaver in the North start from his loom on hearing a pack of hounds and pursue them through a long and fatiguing chase."—Ulster, View halloa![1]

[1] Echoing Arthur Young's *Irish Tour* of 1776–78 "a pack of hounds is never heard, but all the weavers leave their looms, and away they go after them by hundreds."   The hounds are hunting hares.

Agriculture and the Bounty System.

Here the Limerick doctor becomes the respectful critic.

248   He starts with the saving of time by division of labour, as in I, 10 (telescoped, and thus omitting the connotation of "workhouse" in the *Wealth of Nations*—"When the two trades can be carried on in the same workhouse, the loss of time is no doubt much less").

With the farmer-weaver, long so general in Ireland, the health point comes in—

251   "Whether the injuries described by Smith, Young and others to this combination of professions are counter-balanced by the superior health resulting therefrom" is uncertain. (It is in this connection that Eden, in a footnote to his I, 440, refers to Crumpe's Essay.)

There is a hint on 231 of Tenant Right, but it is not developed, perhaps because he did not live in Ulster. "'These customs,' according to Smith, 'so favourable to the yeomanry have contributed more to the present grandeur of England than all the boasted regulations of commerce taken together.'" (I, 367–8.)

Only when a sentence is isolated thus, does one realise how challenging Smithian sentiments could be. Preposterous, and yet how well worth saying!

Bounties.

263   "The utility of bounties has, I know, been arrainged by many, and especially by so respectable an authority as Doctor Smith."

But he answers Smith out of James Anderson, a brother Scot, and makes this good point—

271   "Corn is not the regulating article of subsistence in Ireland."

So he supports the bounty on corn export (Foster's Act of 1784, Irish) on all counts. It increases the supply of corn and the profits of the farmer: it encourages tillage and discourages pasturing.

Commercial Regulations.

Here he quotes Adam Smith on exceptions to free trade (I, 431–2); on linen yarn and poor spinners (II, 142–3); on commerce and the carrying trade (I, 353). And he winds up (360–5) with references to the "Celebrated Commercial Propositions" (of 1785), but to one's disappointment he does not discuss them in any detail. For "they no longer engage the attention of the public." But he is clear on these two points: (1) the commercial self-regulation granted to Ireland in 1782 must not be impaired, (2) "a variety of political reasons . . . strongly demonstrate the necessity of a more strict commercial union" (363). There is no mention of political union; and his last words are "Whether the constitutional defects discovered in them were such as warranted their rejection, this is neither the time nor place to examine."

Crumpe was a doctor concerned for the well-being of the people among whom he lived. He does not preach the Right to Work or the Welfare State, but pins his faith on an economy of full employment achieved within the liberal limits of Smithian self-help. An Irish gem!

The second of our two writers, and, of course, much the better known, is F. M. Eden.

THE STATE OF THE POOR.

Or an History of the Labouring Classes in England from the Conquest to the present period, in which are particularly considered their Domestic Economy with respect to Diet, Dress, Fuel and Habitation, and the various plans for the Relief of the Poor together with Parochial Reports.

By Sir Frederick Morton Eden, Bart.
in 3 volumes.

London, J. Davis, 1797.
—Preface dated at Lincoln's Inn Fields, December, 1796.

F. M. Eden, 1766–1809, the eldest son of Sir Robert Eden, Bart., was the nephew of William Eden, Lord Auckland, and named after William Eden's brother. His work is a classic and, like other classics, has enjoyed the doubtful advantage of reproduction in an abbreviated form. Most of us have had on our shelves the one volume edition by Thorold Rogers' son, A. G. L. Rogers (Routledge, 1928); the father's *magnum opus* being *The History of Agricultural Prices in England A.D.* 1259–1793.

What Eden knew the Rogers knew, and *vice versa* (more or less), and both were grounded on the *Wealth of Nations*.[1] With so ponderous a sub-title, it was inevitable that Eden's work should be known as The State of the Poor, but it is very far from being a History of

[1] J. R. McCulloch, would-be Professor of Political Economy at Edinburgh (1825), and J. E. Thorold Rogers, Drummond Professor of Political Economy at Oxford (1862–67) in turn, 1828 and 1869, edited the *Wealth of Nations*. But neither can compare with the matchless edition of Cannan, and to quote now from these, or any other, is unhelpful.

the Poor Law and Poor Relief.   This enters in, but is quite second-ary.   The treatise is a general survey of the Labouring Classes, of their mode of earning and their mode of life, brought up to the moment of publication and enriched by a wealth of contemporary reports.   The atmosphere is real and tense.   We meet the big wigs—Pitt, Fox, Colquhoun, Count Rumford, and are mobilised for emergency action, for the country was in the crisis of war, with Speenhamland in being and starvation round the corner.   Eden (1797) beat Malthus (1798), but only by a short head.

Towards the end of Volume I he lists the functions of government:

"To prevent the strong from oppressing the weak; to protect the acquisitions of industry, and to check the progress of vice and immor-ality by pointing out and encouraging the instruction of the rising generation in the social and religious duties, to maintain the relations which commerce has created with foreign countries, are duties which require that delegated authority should be exerted by public force, and the vindicatory dispensations of pains and penalties."

But does it foreshadow Malthus and Miss Martineau?   Far from it, and let Karl Marx be our witness here.   In a notable passage of *Das Kapital* he writes:

"Sir F. M. Eden in his *The State of the Poor* (Vol. I, Bk. I, Ch. I) says 'the natural produce of our soil is certainly not fully adequate to our subsistence; we can neither be clothed, lodged, nor fed but in con-sequence of our previous labour.   A portion at least of the society must be indefatigably employed. . . . There are others who, though they "neither toil nor spin," can yet command the produce of industry, but who owe their exemption from labour solely to civilisation and order.   They are peculiarly the creatures of civil institutions,[1] which have recognised that individuals may acquire property by various other means besides the exertion of labour.   Persons of independent fortune owe their superior advantages by no means to any superior abilities of their own, but almost entirely to the industry of others. It is not the possession of land, or of money, but the command of labour which distinguishes the opulent from the labouring part of the community. . . .'   Sir F. M. Eden, it may be remarked in passing, is the only disciple of Adam Smith during the eighteenth century that produced any work of importance."—*Capital*, Ch. XXV, The General Law of Capitalist Accumulation, pp. 628-9.

Strong testimony, but very understandable; for over Eden bridge "labour commanding" passes into "surplus value."

The scheme of Eden's treatise is excellent and fulfils to the letter

[1] Marx disputes this sentiment in a footnote.   Law (he asserts) is a product of the relations of production, and not *vice versa*.

its comprehensive title. It really is a history of the labouring classes, that is to say of those who, when work fails, quickly pass the poverty line. It is with the state of these, the generality of the population, and not of paupers that Eden's *State of the Poor* is concerned. Let us view it in detail.

Vol. I. Bk. I. From the Conquest to the Present Period.

    Ch. I. From the Conquest to the Reformation.

    Ch. II. From the Reformation to the Revolution.

    Ch. III. From the Revolution to the Present.

    Book II.

    Ch. I. Of the Poor Law System.

    Ch. II. Of the Dress, Diet, Fuel and Habitation of the Labouring Classes.

This last is the famous chapter which we have all read (at least in A. G. L. Rogers) and from which endless quotations have been taken. As a Lancashire man newly returned from Newfoundland, I will allow myself just two.

> I, 501. *Potatoes.* "No vegetable is, or ever was, applied to such a variety of uses in the North of England as the potato: it is a constant standing dish at every meal, breakfast excepted, at the tables of the Rich, as well as the Poor. It is generally supposed that they are produced in much greater perfection in Lancashire, and districts near Lancashire, than in other parts of England [cf. W. of N., I, 161]. This, however, I conceive is a mistake. I have indeed eat potatoes there, which, when brought to the table, and touched with a fork, fall into powder, like some of the fungus tribe. Potatoes, however, from the very same field or garden, when sent up to London, appear to be quite a different production: the outside is generally too much done, and is either sodden or watery; while the centre of the potato remains as hard as it was when taken out of the ground."

> I, 532. "Salt fish is now going very generally into disuse. As served, it is hard, dry and unsavoury." But, says Eden, "I remember eating a few years ago at Rome a most exquisite dish of salt fish, millet and sliced potatoes with a very few herbs."

Vol. II. *Parochial Reports.*

These were supplied largely by the clergy of the place, and some of them are exceptionally interesting, especially when they reflect very recent conditions, as this from Portsmouth, Hants.

II, 227.   "The poor of this parish are chiefly maintained in a work-house; in which there are at present about 170 persons who are employed in picking oakum. . . .[1]

The proportion of out-pensioners both in this parish and in Portsea is very inconsiderable: when persons become necessitous the parish generally insists on their going into the workhouse; by which means the expenditure is much reduced; not because the Poor are maintained at a cheaper rate than they could be at their own homes, but because the apprehension of being obliged to intermix with the various kinds of indigent people, usually found in a large Poorhouse, deters many from making applications for relief.   The regulation adopted by the parish, of sending such persons to the work house as are likely to remain chargeable a long time, is a great incitement to industry, and certainly prevents many frivolous claims to parochial assistance: but it seems to bear hard on the modest Poor, who are the most deserving objects of national charity.   The parishes of Portsmouth and Portsea are much at variance: nor will either receive a pauper from the other without an order of removal.   It is said that Portsmouth, in order to reduce its rates, is endeavouring to get incorporated with Portsea: the latter however is determined to oppose this measure.   Both parishes complain of having a great number of Casual Poor.

The high price of provisions is sensibly felt among the labouring classes in this neighbourhood: the quartern loaf of wheaten bread costs 1s.; beef from 6d. to 7d. the lb.; mutton 6d.; veal 8d.; bacon 10½d.; butter 10d. to 15d.; potatoes 5d. the gallon; milk 1d. the pint.   Common labourers earn from 8s. to 10s. a week.   All employments and occupations to any degree connected with the Navy are now actively excited; more especially in His Majesty's dockyards, where there is a great demand for labour; ship-wrights receive standing wages of 6s. 6d. a week, but work double tides (that is, perform double the work usually required) about 2 months in 3, and are then allowed double wages. Besides this they can earn about 2s. 6d. a week by watching, in their turns, at 1s. a night.   Watermen, at present, have constant employment; but in times of peace this class of men is almost starving: tailors, shoe-makers, and other tradesmen, more particularly publicans, are in full business: in short war is the harvest of Portsmouth; and peace, which is so ardently wished for in most other parts of England, is dreaded here."

Oct., 1795.

[1] This dismal device was bettered by William Morton Pitt, long one of Poole's two M.P.'s and later member for the County of Dorset, who, after the death (1835) of the 2nd Earl of Chatham, was the sole male survivor of the Pitt family.   For he established near his place at Purbeck a cordage and sail-cloth factory, as well as a hat factory in Dorchester gaol.

Vol. III completes the Parochial Reports, and concludes with 408 pages of Appendices (21 in all) and an excellent index.   App. 1 is Statistical.   Eden compliments Hume on his interest in prices and quotes the figures of Adam Smith; gives price runs for grain, wool and mutton, a price correction table, as in Folkes, and a mass of isolated prices; reproaching Fleetwood because he does not give the pages or even the names of his authorities; and drawing attention to the snag of "composition price."

> "The sum of 8s., which is mentioned 8 times in the *Chronicon Preciosum*, as the price of wheat between 1444 and 1562, it appears, was a composition price agreed upon between the landlord and the tenant, and continues the same for several years."

(In fact mentioned 10 times between 1551 and 1562, as may be seen by reference to the tables in *Wealth of Nations*, I, 253–4.)   Eden points out further that "the scale of social enjoyment cannot be accurately measured by a collection only of the prices of those commodities which the physical necessities of man require"—the concept of the "civilised minimum."   And of Sunday clothing he says: "Formerly (as Sir John Cullum well observes) we might see at Church, what the cut of a coat was half a century before: no such curiosity is now exhibited, every article of dress is spruce and modern" (*History of Hawsted*, 225).   Sir John Cullum's *The History and Antiquities of Hawsted and Hardwick in the County of Suffolk* served Eden as a model for his national survey.   Cullum was a Fellow of St. Catharine's, Cambridge.

App. No. 10 on the Poor in Scotland is very full, and not surprisingly there is no quotation from Adam Smith here.   But in No. 11, Pitt's Speech on the Poor Relief Bill, February 12, 1796, an indirect allusion to the master is preserved:

> "It was unnecessary (said Pitt) to argue the general expediency of any legislative interference, as the principle had been perfectly recognised by the honble. gentleman [Whitbread] himself.   The most celebrated writers on political economy and the experience of those states whose arts had flourished the most, bore ample testimony of their truth.   They had only to enquire therefore whether the present case was strong enough for the exception. . . ."

Eden, like Adam Smith, stood boldly for self-help, but he was not blind to the virtue of self-help through association, and Appendix 20, Table of Friendly Society Contributions and Allowances for Sickness and Old Age, valuable in itself, is of biographical value also, seeing that Eden was co-founder and managing chairman of the Globe

Insurance Society, 1st Meeting, Monday, April 15, 1803, Sir Frederick Morton Eden, Bart., being present and appointed Chairman. Hence the significance in the main text *sub* London of

> "These [safety] provisions have been considerably enlarged by the Building Act (14 Geo. 3 c 78 [Fire Prevention, Metropolis]), the enforcing of which (there can be no doubt) has greatly contributed towards the health, the safety, and the beauty, of the Metropolis."

But does the treatise really stand up to its sub-title, History of the Labouring Classes in England?   Surely.   Consider only the following from Bk. I, Ch. I:—

I, 41. "I consider the regulation of wages as a device confessedly framed by the nobility, and, if not intended, certainly tending, to cramp the exertions of industry. Great proprietors, who, in their zeal to participate in the conveniences and elegancies offered them by commerce, had gradually relinquished their arbitrary rights over the persons of their dependents, for a pecuniary equivalent, which enabled them to exchange the riotous hospitality of a castle, for the less turbulent, though no less expensive, splendor of the court and the capital, must soon have discovered, that a man acquired if not additional bodily strength, at least an additional spur to industry from emancipation: they must have seen the strong allurements held out, both by commerce and manufacture, to the idle occupiers of their manors; and have felt, that the various pretexts for enfranchisement, supported by the subtleties of the courts of justice, would, in the end, had they not been resisted, lead to the utter extinction of villenage. The new system of working for hire, which was gradually making its way, was, no doubt, more profitable to them, and more conducive to national prosperity, than the labour of slaves: but it may be doubted whether this political truth (not universally assented to, even in the present age), that the labour of free hands is more productive to the employer than the service of slaves, was, in that unenlightened period, understood, or voluntarily practised, by great proprietors; and if they could not comprehend the beneficial effects of this important revolution, we cannot be surprised, that they should endeavour to preserve some affinity between the new class of labourers and the old class of villeins, by limiting their earnings, as they had before controuled their persons. All the restrictions of the Legislature, on personal industry, evince a disposition of this kind; the various statutes to regulate wages, dress and apparel, seem to have been framed with the same view; namely, to curb the aspiring exertions of industry and independency."

I, 56. . . . "The desire of bettering our condition, which is the predominant principle that animates the world, and which, when expanded into action, gives birth to every social virtue, would alike have impelled the lord to prefer comfort to splendor, and the villein to quit his livery for the independence of trade: and it was happy for mankind, that these exchanges produced essential advantages, not only to the lord and vassal, but to the community at large. A man who, by dismissing half of his useless domestics, purchased the means of adding to his enjoyments; who could therefore clothe himself in woollen and fine linen, instead of coarse canvas and a leathern jerkin, or jacket; who could add the wholesome and grateful productions of horticulture to his table; and could render a dreary castle more habitable by substituting warm hangings for bare stone, or at most white-washed walls; and that elegant conveniency, glass, for latticed windows; would act conformably to principles, which are not more natural to the masters, than to the labouring part of mankind."

I, 59. "Dr. Johnson's remark, on marriage and celibacy, may, perhaps, be applied with propriety to freedom and servitude: the one has many pains; the other no pleasures.—*Rasselas*."[1]

(But better still a life-pension of £400 a year; for that, as Hume told Adam Smith, when he got his, October, 1765, meant "opulence and liberty," with no pains attached (*New Letters, op. cit.*, p. 131). Well said, David; and as touching slavery, add this—If a poor slave were inventive, he "instead of reward, would probably meet with much abuse, perhaps with some punishment" (*W. of N.*, II, 182).)

I, 61. "To complain, however, that they [manufactures and commerce] have, by the inequality which industry must occasion, been the source of misery to some members of the community, is to complain of the causes which have raised us to an unexampled pitch of national prosperity and of the consequences which are necessarily attached to it."

This, to be sure, is, in a measure, "conjectural" history, and it echoes plainly the "pair of diamond buckles" and "mess of pottage" passages in the *Wealth of Nations* (I, 387, 389). But, as in Adam Smith's Book III, on which it is modelled, theory is steadied by illustration from history, as the argument proceeds. Thus:

I, 55. ". . . Such are the metayers of France; a species of tenant, which Adam Smith (who has traced with admirable precision, the various gradations of tenantry, from the servile cultivator of ancient times, the fruits of whose industry were at the disposal of his master, to the independent modern farmer, whose lease affords him equal security with his landlord), observes,

---

[1] Which in Jane Austen becomes: "though Mansfield Park might have some pains, Portsmouth could have no pleasures."

has been long in disuse in England"—with footnote reference
to W. of N., 5th ed., II, 90, which in Cannan is I, 365.

We established the discipleship of Samuel Crumpe by listing all
the references to the *Wealth of Nations*. To do this with Eden
would make a view of him inconveniently long.   In the main text
and the voluminous footnotes there are a score and more of references, and some long quotations, running to hundreds of words.
Two samples must suffice, the first illustrating a topic on which
Adam Smith writes with emphasis, and Eden with fuller knowledge,
namely the law of Poor Settlement.

I, 175. "By the 13th & 14th of Charles the second [c 12] it was
enacted, that the residence in a parish, necessary in order to
produce a settlement, should be reduced to 40 days, and that,
within that time, it should be lawful for any two Justices of
the Peace upon complaint made by the churchwardens and
overseers of the Poor, to remove any newcomer to the parish
where he was last legally settled, either as a native, house-
holder, sojourner, apprentice, or servant, for the space of 40
days in the least, unless he either rented a tenement of £10 a
year (*footnote*.—The reason of fixing £10 a year is because it
requires such a stock that the man is not to be presumed
likely to become chargeable, *Burrow's select cases* 10), or
could give such security for the discharge of the parish, where
he was living, as the two Justices should deem sufficient.
This single clause of a short act of parliament has occasioned
more doubts and difficulties in Westminster Hall, and has
(perhaps) been more profitable to the Profession of the Law,
than any other point in English Jurisprudence."

I, 178. "An English labourer is now authorised to remain, in any
place where he may choose for his residence, till he becomes
actually chargeable—35 Geo. 3 c. 101."

I, 181. "Of the inconveniences occasioned by the Law of Settlements,
Adam Smith, and Lord Kames, have spoken in very energetic
(and in most instances, very just), terms of reprobation. . . .
To remove a man, who has committed no misdemeanor, from
the parish where he chooses to reside, is an evident violation
of natural liberty and justice, an oppression, to which the
people of England, though jealous of their liberty, but like
the peoples of most other countries, never rightly considering
in what it consists, have for more than a century together,
suffered themselves to be exposed to this oppression without
a remedy." [Based on *Wealth of Nations*, I, 142.]   Neither
of these writers, however seem to be warranted by fact in
their supposition, that the price of labour, in their own
country, is from its absence in Scotland far more equal than
it is in England."

I, 297. "I am far from agreeing with Mr. Hay, who supposes that these oppressions were very generally practised; or believing, as Adam Smith seems to think, that 'there is scarce a poor man of England of 40 years of age, who has not in some part of his life felt himself most cruelly oppressed by the Law of Settlements.' [*Ibid.*] 'Their operation,' as Mr. Howlett justly remarks, 'has been very trifling indeed. How seldom do the young and healthy, while single, find any difficulty in changing their residence, and fixing where they please.'"

On the actual working of the Apprenticeship and Corporation Laws, again with copious references to the *Wealth of Nations*, Eden is equally full, but let this, with its shrewd critique, suffice:—

Vol. I, Bk. I, 436. "Adam Smith, indeed, asserts, 'that in many large incorporated towns, no tolerable workmen are to be found, even in some of the most necessary trades.' 'If you would have your work tolerably executed,' he says, 'it must be done in the suburbs, where the workmen, having no exclusive privilege, have nothing but their character to depend upon, and you must then smuggle it into the town as well as you can.' [*Wealth of Nations*, I, 131.] It is much to be regretted that this great political writer did not provide any evidence of the truth of these asseverations. I confess I very much doubt whether there is a single corporation in England, the exercise of whose rights does, at present, operate in this manner. The truth seems to be, that corporations are themselves sensible that commerce no longer needs their protection, and that the exercise of their privileges in driving an industrious stranger from the sphere of their jurisdiction would chiefly affect their own interests. In this instance, as in many others, the insensible progress of society has reduced chartered rights . . . to a state of inactivity."

True enough in its day, but there are other rights than chartered rights, the rights namely of human beings. Therefore the understanding and correction of the psychological impact of mass employment in great towns on the skilled worker's will to work (or to set up for himself) has become, in our machine age, the central problem of industrial management: here, surely, Adam Smith was prescient. Finally, note the standing of the authorities here adduced:

Sir James Burrow, 1701–82, some time President of the Royal Society, issued excellent Law Reports, notably one on Copyright.
William Hay, 1695–1755, lawyer of the Middle Temple, a Sussex man and observant traveller, published "Remarks on Laws relating to the Poor, 1735."[1]

[1] See Cannan's footnote on I, 142, linking Hay with Smith and Eden.

John Howlett, 1731–1804, a political economist of Oxford and the vicar of Great Dunmow, dealt in his Miscellaneous writings with Population and the Poor Law.

Again and again Eden's authorities are men of D.N.B. stature; and not the least among the treasures of his noble work is Appendix No. 18, a bibliography, chronological, of the relevant English literature, with 282 entries. It should be the aim of every university, with an economics department, to possess a copy of the three-volume edition; and someone surely should give us a worthy life of Sir Frederick Morton Eden, Bart., the great grandfather of our late Prime Minister. For this there is ample material, in particular in the archives of the "Royal-Globe" in Liverpool and London. It is a truism to say that Adam Smith dominated the fiscal policy of nineteenth-century Britain. But Ricardo and Malthus, the one with his Iron Law of Wages, the other with the Essay on Population, dominated—unhappily—the social thinking of their age. For they made (with female assistance) Political Economy the "dismal science," from which at length it was rescued by the genius of Jevons and Marshall.

When Marshall was equipping me, in 1907–08, to lecture on history and theory to first year students in the Economics Tripos, he surprised me by saying:

(i) That I must read Adam Smith from beginning to end, especially Book V. It took me years to find out, why Book V.

(ii) That in his opinion the mathematical treatment was now much overdone (a sentiment which I hastened to pass on to his successor).

(iii) That after long years of thought he had come to the conclusion that in the great currency controversy of Tooke versus Ricardo, Tooke was more right than Ricardo, in token whereof he lent me for the space of 6 years (i.e. to the outbreak of World War I) his second copy of Tooke's *History of Prices*, then a rare six-volume work.

Chapter III

EARLY YEARS OF THE
GLASGOW CHAMBER OF COMMERCE

(By courtesy of the Directors of the Glasgow Chamber of Commerce)

STRUCTURE AND PURPOSE—PATRICK COLQUHOUN, JOHN PALMER, DAVID DALE—COMMERCIAL REFORMS—HOSTILITY TO CORN LAWS.

"I expect," wrote Adam Smith to a French friend on November 1, 1785, "all the bad consequences from the Chambers of Commerce and Manufacture, establishing in different parts of this country, which Your Grace seems to foresee. In a country where clamour always intimidates and faction often oppresses the Government, the regulations of commerce are commonly dictated by those who are most interested to deceive and impose upon the public."

("Your Grace" is Le Duc de la Rochefoucauld. In the Athenaeum of 28/12/1895, John Rae gives the letter in full; and the cutting from this weekly is pinned to James Bonar's copy of Rae's *Life of Adam Smith* in Glasgow University Library.)

The Glasgow Chamber of Commerce was founded in 1783, and down to the end of 1785 there was nothing in its record to make him doubt the truth of his prognostication. Yet before his death in 1790 he had received from it the fullest endorsement of his policy that was to be given by any body of business men during the next 30 years.

The Minutes, intact from 1783, are in the Chamber's Board Room, Merchants House Building, George Square, Glasgow, where hangs the portrait of its founder, Patrick Colquhoun. There are also portraits of Gilbert Hamilton (by Raeburn) and Dugald Bannatyne (by J. G. Gilbert), and on a stand is a small bust in bronze of King Henry IV of France, who "in 1600 founded the Marseilles Chamber of Commerce." Gilbert Hamilton (1744–1809) was Lord Provost of Glasgow 1792–93; Director and first Secretary of the Chamber 1783–1809. Dugald Bannatyne (1755–1842) was Deputy Chairman 1792–93 and Secretary 1809–42. In the entrance hall is the statue of Kirkman Finlay (1773–1842), who in 1812 was both Lord Provost of Glasgow and its M.P., in 1819 Rector of Glasgow University, the trusted friend of John Gladstone and William Huskisson, and in truth the uncrowned king of Glasgow commerce for a generation. He was Chairman of the Chamber 1812–13, 1816–17, 1829–30.

Conditori Patricio de Colquhoun the inscription to the portrait reads in its place of honour above the mantlepiece. When I was an undergraduate of King's a New Zealand friend of mine and fellow historian reached the final of the Colquhoun Sculls (1903), so easy to pronounce—Cohoon—though rather difficult to spell. Later as a young don I picked up second hand copies of the *Police of the Metropolis* (1806) and the *Treatise on the Wealth, Power and Resources of the British Empire* (1815), the statistical bible of the Early English Socialists—both by Patrick Colquhoun, LL.D. I used to lecture on the former in relation to the London Docks and the Thames River Police, which he organised: on the latter in relation to Robert Owen, Dale's son-in-law, the father of socialism. Unfortunately, however, when finishing in Canada my text book on *Great Britain from Adam Smith to the Present Day*, I made Patrick Colquhoun a Sir, by confusion with his great-grandson Sir Patrick Macchombaich Colquhoun, the famous oarsman of Lady Margaret, Cambridge and founder (1835) of the Sculls. I am not certain whether I committed thus a prochronism or a parachronism. The simpler term, perhaps, is "howler."

In its first years the Chamber met in the Tontine Tavern; and on January 1, 1783, with Colquhoun in the chair, the "heads of a plan" were adopted. There were three grades of subscription: a few at 20 guineas; rather more at 10; the majority at 5. All the well-known names of Glasgow commerce are there—Jamieson, Robertson, Robison, Black, Buchanan, Bogle, Dunlop, Finlay, Henderson, Mitchell; and it was intriguing, after a perusal of the list, to go to Ramshorn Burying Ground in the old part of the town and read there many of the same names—their own or that of their father.

The purpose of the Chamber was declared to be the furtherance of commerce and manufacture, but in addition "the Directors are to accept of arbitrations in disputes upon mercantile cases, in order to save the heavy expenses attending law suits." Its work was done by committees, reporting to the general meeting; and the reports, when approved, were printed and circulated to members of Parliament, other Chambers of Commerce, and influential persons. I have seen several in the Board of Trade Papers (P.R.O.). Furthermore, liaison was maintained with the Trustees for Fisheries and Manufactures.

Upon the return of peace in 1783, tobacco smuggling became once more an urgent problem, and the traders and manufacturers of Glasgow resolved to boycott dealers in the smuggled article, which elicited, September 23, 1783, an approval from the Custom House at Edinburgh, concluding:

"Assuring you of our most hearty concurrence to so desirable an end and every assistance that the laws will allow of, towards the punishment of all offenders.

Signed . . . Basil Cocharane
Adam Smith
Jas. Buchanan."

Another urgency was better communications, endorsed in advance by the Master. "Good roads, canals, and navigable rivers, by diminishing the expence of carriage, put the remote parts of the country more nearly upon a level with those in the neighbourhood of the town. They are upon that account the greatest of all improvements" (*Wealth of Nations*, I, 148).

Roads, especially for passengers and mail. In 1784 the Chamber was complaining that Glasgow letters came via Edinburgh, so that when the London mail was late it had to be forwarded by special expresses. But on October 14, 1788, it was able to thank John Palmer, Esq., Surveyor and Comptroller General of His Majesty's Mails, for the extension of the London-Carlisle service to Glasgow, and resolved:

That the Chamber will do everything in their power by themselves and their friends to support the mail coach, and to countenance and encourage those inn-keepers that run it and perform their duty with regularity.

This was that John Palmer of Bath who in the face of official opposition had established the practicability of carrying the mails by stage coach, with a consequent increase of 50 per cent in the Post Office revenue between 1784 and 1787.

Canals. The Forth and Clyde Canal, constructed in full, 1768–90, extends from the Forth at Grangemouth to the Clyde at Bowling; and it was Scotland's main *industrial* canal, for the carriage of minerals and foodstuffs. In 1788 the Chamber had a grievance against it.

The Forth and Clyde navigation is rendered useless to the Trade and Commerce of the Country from the absurd regulations which prevail with regard to the transit of many articles, where the expence of

Custom House dispatches, added to the Tonnage dues, raise the price above the standard of Land Carriage, altho' independently of such dispatches, the expence is not above one half.

And what was even worse:

> By placing the entrance to the canal at Grangemouth [on the Forth, W. of Bo'ness], out of the district of Glasgow, inconceivable hardships and inconveniences result to the dealers in grain imported from foreign parts; as on account of this trifling circumstance vessels have not been permitted to break bulk, or unload into lighters proceeding up to Glasgow, merely because Grangemouth is in the District of Borrowstonness [Bo'ness], and the County of Stirling is not, perhaps, at the very time open for the importation of grain.   And thus it has recently happened that vessels loaded with grain, lying within 20 miles distance . . . have been compelled to circumnavigate half the Island . . . at a great additional expence in assurance, freight and risk of damage by heating and boisterous weather.

For the problems caused by the taking of average price by Maritime Districts, 12 for England, 4 for Scotland, see my *Corn Laws and Social England*, 63–4.

The canal grievance was part of a larger one, the excess of Custom House charges and formalities, which it was the principal task of Pitt and Huskisson to ameliorate.

> It will scarce be credited that in the simple operation of importing, warehousing, and again exporting a single hogshead of tobacco, the marks, numbers and weights are written over by the different officers and clerks at least 25 times; and so multiplied and vexatious are the forms now in practice that the process of paying up the duty of a single hogshead generally exhausts several hours.
> The proving of goods for export requires the joint presence of Customs and Excise.   The trouble and difficulty of collecting the two setts of officers together is not to be conceived.

But if fees were abolished and duties reduced, what was to take their place?   Here Glasgow was not so helpful.   They had opposed in 1784–85 the imposition of excise duties on printed linen, cotton and silk, preferring (vaguely) "a system of taxation that shall rest upon consumption alone, without disturbing a valuable manufacture in its progress to maturity."   But where was the machinery for such a tax on consumption?   And Pitt, later, in the stress of major war, had to feel his way to an Income Tax without help either from Glasgow or the *Wealth of Nations*.

The Glasgow Chamber opposed also Pitt's Irish Proposals in 1785, on the ground that they gave Ireland, Scotland's competitor in the linen industry, "advantages without burdens." But it supported warmly the French Treaty of 1786, in a Minute of January 24, 1787:

> We are of opinion that by authorising an interchange of the best products of either country upon easy duties, it will imperceptibly direct the industry of each to its natural and most beneficial channels and more effectually promote the interest of both.

This change of heart rested on change of substance; for France then gave more than she got; the ban on her silk goods remained, and her domestic industry was unfitted to compete with the machine-made textiles of Britain, which were setting the industrial pace in the Lancashire of Arkwright and Crompton, and the Lanarkshire of David Dale and Robert Owen. David Dale became Deputy Chairman of the Chamber in 1786, and the Minute of 1787 was Glasgow's vote of confidence in the founder of Scotland's new cotton industry. Shortly after, Colquhoun left for London, to act there as the Chamber's commercial agent and become a Metropolitan Magistrate.

At this point the Corn Laws enter into the picture. A warning to members was sounded in January, 1787, provoked by the proposal of certain "landed gentlemen who met at Edinburgh in August last." Glasgow replied by ordering a detailed enquiry into Corn Law history, "from the Revolution [of 1688] to the present time"; and this done, drew up a general report in 1788, repudiating the time-honoured policy of export bounties, and finally, on March 15, 1790, a special report resting avowedly on the new teaching in the *Wealth of Nations*. The Report opens:

> A much and justly celebrated living author [he died that July] has proposed the true and only radical means of removing all the evils and inconveniences complained of, namely, the repeal of the whole system of Corn Laws, and establishment of a perfect freedom of trade in that essential necessary of life. . . .

The Report was approved, and three weeks later, April 9, 1700, a supplement was added which rounded off the issue:

> It has, in our humble opinion, been demonstrated that no benefit worth counting on has been derived from the Bounty, even to the Corn counties; as the chief effect of it must have been to enhance the price to the consumer, and of course to raise that of every species of manufacture and other article of consumption, so that the farmers and landholders lose first; while on the other hand every circumstance, which enhances the price of our manufactures, must limit our powers of competition in foreign markets, where the bounty on exportation enables their manufacturers to eat our corn on equal and sometimes lower terms than we do ourselves. It has ever been accounted wise

policy in a manufacturing nation, to encourage the importation of the raw materials of their manufacturers on as low terms as possible; but this has been entirely lost sight of in the instance before us; as the direct tendency of the Bounty and many of our Corn Regulations is artificially to enhance the price of the most necessary and important of all materials—the bread and subsistence of our labourers and manufacturers.

It may be proper here to take notice of a remark mentioned by their Lordships [of the Council for Trade] that in manufacturing towns there is more regularity of conduct and more productive industry when corn is not at a price unusually low. This sobriety and industry, however, is not to be imputed to such price being high, but to its being correspondent to that medium value on which the price of labour must be computed; as manufacturers and all other labourers are uniformly found most sober and industrious, when their wages are sufficient to make them live comfortably without admitting of idleness or dissipation. In this country, therefore, where the value of corn is, by the force of the Regulations, kept above its natural rate, the medium on which wages must be computed is necessarily proportionately high, and the labourers and manufacturers will, of course, be found most sober and industrious when the price of corn corresponds to that rather high medium rate. But if the price of corn were not thus artificially kept up, the medium would be lowered, the wages of labour, of course, would be reduced and the manufacturers would be found equally sober and industrious, when the actual price of corn corresponded to this low medium, as when it at present corresponds to the high one, with this important difference that the articles would come proportionately cheaper to the consumer at home, and go with infinitely more advantage into the competition in foreign markets.

But tho' the country, whose corn and of course the wages of labour are correspondingly low, has thus (other things being equal) so great and obvious advantage over all others, where these are higher, yet the sobriety and industry of the manufacturers, while they have employment, does not depend so much on the medium to which their wages correspond being comparatively high or low as on the actual prices being steadily kept at or about that medium wherever it may be.

It thus becomes clear that when Thomas Tooke, the Baltic merchant and historian of Prices, invited his readers to suppose that the Free Trade Movement started with the London Merchants' Petition of 1820, drafted by himself, he was indulging in fiction. He did not start it: he only re-started, after a generation of war, a movement which had been launched in the 1780's from commercial centres in the industrial north, of which the voice from Adam Smith's university town was the most emphatic and the most precise.

Let Glasgow flourish.

CHAPTER IV

TIMBER

COMMODITY STUDY—WOOD AND COAL—THE CARRYING TRADE—
BALTIC TIMBER AND GRAIN—NAVIGATION ACT—FROM ADAM SMITH
TO COBDEN.

Scope of Survey

"To feed well, old Cato said, as we are told by Cicero, was the
first and most profitable thing in the management of a private
estate; to feed tolerably well, the second; and to feed ill, the third.
To plough, he ranked only in the fourth place of profit and advantage."—*W. of N.*, I, 151.
For "feed" read "browse," for "plough" read "plough through
current periodicals"; and that goes for this which follows.

TIMBER . TOBACCO . COAL

Like Caesar's Gaul, our Survey is divided into three parts: something on timber, something on tobacco, and much finally on coal—
making chapters IV, V and VI-VII. We view the whole (by favour
of King's Beam House) through the spy-glass of His Majesty's
Customs at Newcastle, Sunderland and Swansea, and let it be said,
here and now, there were few things which escaped their vigilant eye.

Newcastle: the Pons Aelii of the Romans, the Novum Castellum
Super Tinam of Post Conquest England.

Sunderland: the *sunder*, *separate*, land of the Abbey of Jarrow,
where Bede was born.

Swansea called by the Welsh Abertawe: Swansea itself being
conjecturally "Swein's eie" (Swein's island) after a Norse settler of
that name, though, like Pepys Island in the South Atlantic, no such
island existed.

Wealth of Nations, I, 23.

"There are in Africa none of those great inlets, such as the Baltic and
Adriatic seas in Europe . . . to carry maritime commerce into the
interior parts of that great continent."

And any Canadian who reads this will add for himself "such, too,
as the St. Lawrence and Great Lakes."

Ibid., I, 164, 167.

"The woods of Norway and of the coasts of the Baltic find a market in
many parts of Great Britain which they could not find at home, and
thereby afford some rent to the proprietors."

"Upon the sea-coast of a well improved country, indeed, if coals can be conveniently had for fewel, it may sometimes be cheaper to bring barren timber for building from less cultivated foreign countries than to raise it at home. In the new town of Edinburgh, built within these last few years, there is not, perhaps, a single stick of Scotch timber."

Cf. the Diary of Sir Walter Scott, in Lockhart's *Life*, Ch. 74, for October 7, 1827 (after his visit to Sir Cuthbert Sharp, Collector at Sunderland):

"All that the Duke [of Northumberland] cuts down [at Alnwick] is so much waste, for the people will not buy it where coals are so cheap."

But it was otherwise in the Italy of Fra Colonna—on authority infallible. "Fox! They will not burn thee; wood is too dear" (*The Cloister and the Hearth*, Ch. 62).

Newcastle Collector to "Hon Sirs" [Customs Commissioners], London, January, 1730:

"The *Rachel* of Portsmouth from Dantzick, laden with wheat flour and oatmeal for the Garrison at Gibraltar,[1] as she was coming into this Harbour, was stranded upon the Rock a little below Tinmouth Castle. They have got most of the wheat and flour landed, are drying it, and the rock being thro' the ship in several places, they desire to ship it aboard another ship for Gibraltar."

1742.

"Copenhagen beechwood blocks since 20 years used by coal owners for making wheels of coal waggons but not so durable as English oak. The price therefore has dropped to a half."

Thus, 1730 introduces us to the sequence (repeated in Canada) of grain, timber, grain; and 1742 heralds at a distance George Stephenson's locomotive engine, carrying coals on an iron railroad. (From Newcastle Central Station the entrance to the Railway Age is simplicity itself. You cross with caution to the island which carries the statue of George Stephenson, facing east, and mark around him the four recumbent figures, presenting his Grand Allies—Puffing Billy; a miner, with hammer, stripped to the waist; the Humphry Davy safety lamp; and the iron rail.)

1744. Entry of bars of iron consigned to Mr. Joseph Airey, Merchant and Agent to John Ambrose Crowley. Bars are Swedish, and the works agent says that

"Mr. Crowley is under contract to supply the Navy with anchors, and was obliged to purchase this and a large parcel of Barr in Holland

1 Captured in 1704 by Admiral Sir George Rooke.

in order to perform their contract with the expedition required by he Navy Office, which they could not have done if they had sent for it to Sweden."

The Navigation Acts prohibited the importation of Baltic materials from Holland or in Dutch ships, as measures of policy against the Dutch carrying trade. Carrying did not necessarily mean carrying *for others*; though, as Adam Smith surmises, I, 351:

> "The trade itself has probably derived its name from it, the people of such countries [as Holland] being the carriers to other countries. . . . It is upon this account, however, that the carrying trade has been supposed peculiarly advantageous to such a country as Great Britain, of which the defence and security depend upon the number of its sailors and shipping."

1757. Imports of wheat and rye from Dantzick.

1769.

"It is too much the practice at this port (which is countenanced by that of the Port of London) for vessels trading to the Baltic and Hambro' to go out as bare as possible of Cables and Cordage, in order to supply themselves with those articles, which they can do at a much easier rate than in this Kingdom, seeing that the payment of the duties is evaded by the pretence of Necessity for the Ship's use, which is so far from being the case in general that the cables are sometimes only just dip't in the water that they may have the appearance of having been used."

1773. A seizure of masts for not paying the proper duty.

At this period the Mersey was regarded by the East Coast as a timber upstart. In 1785, Newcastle accuses Liverpool of under-charging the timber duties, and the Deputy Controller remembers hearing, when he was a clerk at Hull in 1764, that it was doing ditto then.

1782–1801 (peace 1783–93; war 1793–1801).

Numerous entries, year by year, of such materials as:—

Tar, turpentine, spars, axle-trees, handspikes; deals, raff, battens. (As terms, these last three denoted different sorts or lengths of timber. In etymology, deal = plank or floor; raff, cf. rafter; batten, cf. baton.) Outstandingly from Norway.

Firs, spruce, wheat, rye from Dantzick and Memel.

Pitch, tar, hemp, timber from St. Petersburg. (If I were more familiar with the Mediterranean, I might say something about the ancestry of that "best Slavonian oak," which Messrs. Prime quoted some years ago for the new bookcase in King's College, Cambridge, library, but I lack John Galt's knowledge here.)

Iron from Sweden, with frequent disputes over "new" or "old" and how to "admeasure" the various qualities—a pressing reason for its unhampered admission during the Napoleonic War was to prevent it falling into enemy hands.

We turn to Sunderland, and in particular to their letters *from* London.

1766, October.

"Copy of a letter from Mr. [Edmund] Burke, Secretary to Mr. Conway,[1] with an extract from Mr. Gunning, Resident at Copenhagen, notifying the sales there, ending last week," of East Indian teas and China wares. These are "brought up for smuggling into England, some to be run, others to be shipped on small vessels apparently loaded with timber, which cruise about the Islands of Jersey and Guernsey, till signals are made from thence of those Coasts being clear. On the appearance of a Revenue Cruiser, they sail into a French port under pretext of revictualling."

Cf. Newcastle, 1773, on the practice of armed shallops:

"to lay on the track of the colliers, and dispose of their goods by their boats. Small vessels fetch the goods from Dunkirk and then return for more"—to "lay by," as we say of motor lorries.

Bohea tea figures frequently.

1767. Gothenburg tea sales. Two ships thence have cleared for Madeira, but much suspected to be bound no further than our own coast. Watch out for these. (And there are periodic instructions of equal urgency, based on consular reports, notifying the outbreak of plague in Mediterranean Waters: to which Sir William Hamilton and Horace Walpole's correspondent, Sir Horace Mann, eagerly contributed.) Has the *Wealth of Nations* anything to say here? Yes.

---

[1] H. S. Conway was Secretary of State, Southern Department, July 10, 1765, to May, 1766, and Northern Department, May 23, 1766, to January 20, 1768. On August 16, 1765, he communicated to Hume the despatch of Hugh Palliser, Governor of Newfoundland, on which Hume based his mémoire to the French Ministry of Foreign Affairs, complaining of encroachments on the reserved fishery of the S. and S.W. coasts of Newfoundland, military fortifications in St. Pierre, contrary to treaty, and the disquite caused by the coastal cruising of a French man of war of 50 guns in the St. Lawrence.—*New Letters of David Hume, op. cit.*, 223–5.

I, 405.

> "All the sanguinary laws of the customs are not able to prevent the importation of the teas of the Dutch and Gottenburgh East India companies; because somewhat cheaper than those of the British company."

Newcastle Customs from 1759 onwards furnished returns of shipping, British and Foreign, Inwards and Outwards. The crucial figures are British ships outwards. They reveal the predominance of the Baltic trade and the unique position of Denmark, of which Norway was then a political part. Of 187 ships clearing outwards (year ending January 5, 1759), 69 cleared for Denmark, 48 for Germany, 18 for Holland, 4 each for Norway and Sweden. In January 5, 1765, the Seven Years War being ended, France enters the list, coming third to Denmark and Germany. The aggregate of trade grew steadily in the second half of the century: Germany after January, 1769, leading Denmark. (These figures of British ships, clearing outwards for the countries named, only give a part, though the major part, of the shipments, inwards and outwards, under all flags.) Gothenburg, at the entrance of the Kattegat, was the principal port of Sweden, and for England a key port in the last decade of the Napoleonic War, say 1803–13. South of it was Copenhagen in the Sound, the London-cum-Portsmouth of Denmark, and bitterly hostile to England after Canning's seizure of her fleet in 1807. Midway between these two ports lay the Island of Anhalt garrisoned in the final years of the war by British troops. As in North America (1812–15), the tie-in between naval power and trade protection was of the first significance: and the fiscal policy of Huskisson, 1815–30—lower tariffs all round with imperial preference, notably for Canadian timber, together with shipping reciprocities, from which, in fact, Norway (now attached to Sweden) gained more than Britain[1]—was the direct outcome of a generation of major war.

> "As defence, however, is of much more importance than opulence, the act of navigation is, perhaps, the wisest of all the commercial regulations of England. (I, 429.)

Note the adjective "commercial." And therefore in modifying the time-honoured code Huskisson observed the caveat of his doctrinal master by reserving inter-imperial trade to British and colonial shipping. We must not say that in Adam Smith's view the Navigation Acts were strategically sound and economically wrong; for that

---

[1] Cf. L. A. Harper, *The English Navigation Laws*, 352–3.

is to make nonsense of Economic Policy. If you would get into his mind here, read John Selden's *Mare clausum* of 1635. We have at Queen's, Belfast, Adam Smith's copy, with his book plate in it, a superb folio (in Latin) bound up in brown calf with other treatises on Sea Power, including the Intercursus Magnus of 1496 between Henry VII and Philip Duke of Burgundy.

Above all, do not belittle him (necessarily without a shred of evidence) by suggesting that the project of empire in his peroration was a sort of *reductio ad absurdum*. The conflict between the two "Utopias," of Free Trade, I, 435, and of Colonial Representation (with a proportionate share in the burden of taxation), II, 419; the conflict, at bottom, between consumers' plenty and sea-faring strength, runs through Books IV and V. And the possible reconciliation of the two in terms of empire was the master-thought of the world's greatest economist.

One could hardly call Richard Cobden a militarist, yet he was (to coin a necessary word) a "navalist." For on February 20, 1865, within a few weeks of his death on April 2, he expresses himself to Gladstone thus—After pronouncing Canada north of the Great Lakes "almost all forest, with a most rigorous climate," and unlikely ever to attract immigrants from the country south of the border, "with its almost illimitable extent of prairie lands, underlaid generally with coal and other minerals"; this Canada incapable, withal, for geographical reasons, of being successfully defended by British troops, he concludes:

"I attach as much importance as anyone to the maintenance of our naval strength, which, as I have again and again said in Parliament, must be 50 per cent greater than that of any other power, which, like ourselves, is at peace."

(Gladstone Papers, British Museum Add. 44,136, folio 262.)

Thus Adam Smith and Richard Cobden, the chief apostles of free trade, join hands over the century.

CHAPTER V

TOBACCO

CLANDESTINE BORDER TRAFFIC—IMPACT ON NEWCASTLE—HIGH-
WAYMEN—TOBACCO AND THE EXCISE—RE-EXPORT TRADE TO
FRANCE—SMITH AND SMOLLETT.

"It's board and lodging to me, is smoke."

At the Magpie and Stump it was cigars, but speaking with the
voice of 1960, *Player's Please* and in Belfast *Ask for Blues*—tho',
to be sure, rival solicitations grow yearly.

Wealth of Nations, I, 148.

"Good roads, canals and navigable rivers, by diminishing the expence
of carriage, put the remote parts of the country more nearly upon
a level with those in the neighbourhood of the town.   They are upon
that account the greatest of all improvements."

The tobacco lords in scarlet cloaks were alive to this: it is even
possible that they prompted the thought, so far, at least, as roads
went.

We have had this passage already under Glasgow Chamber of
Commerce, but it serves here as our tobacco text because the
economies of Scotland and England were shaped towards integration
by the Union of 1707.   Yet it is not a question of Highland kelp
reaching the corn lands of Yorkshire or of Hebridean herring selling
on the fish markets of Newcastle and Carlisle, but of the internal
movement of a commodity prohibited to be grown at home and
imported wholly from across the Atlantic.

Therefore the basic thought can recur under a country so different
as China, whose sovereigns, we are reminded on II, 322, are said:

"to have been extremely attentive to the making and maintaining of
good roads and navigable canals, in order to increase, as much as
possible, both the quantity and value of every part of the produce of
the land, by procuring to every part of it the most extensive market
which their own dominions could afford."

A half-way house, perhaps, to the Open Door?   On the contrary.
"The Chinese have little respect for foreign trade.   Your beggarly
commerce! was the language" they used concerning it (II, 178).

1749. Newcastle to London.

"Dealers in Tobacco here, who formerly used to have it from London, have for about 15 years past [i.e. since 1734, when A.S. was at Kirkcaldy Burgh School under David Millar] had it from Scotland and Whitehaven, but chiefly from Scotland, and they have heard some of the merchants say that they could have the same tobacco delivered to them here cheaper than they could buy it at London, and that great quantities have for several years past been brought and still continue to be brought by land from Scotland, from which there is reason to believe that frauds must have been committed."

1750. Between 1748 and 1751 A.S. was delivering his Edinburgh lectures, from which the following sentence—photostat in W. R. Scott, *Adam Smith as Student and Professor*, 383—is taken:

"If there was no other communication, therefore, between Edinburgh and London but by land, as no goods could be transported from the one place to the other except such whose price was very high in proportion to their weight, there could not be the hundredth part of the commerce which is at present carried on between them, nor, in consequence, the hundredth part of the encouragement which they at present mutually give to each other's industry.[1]

"Now the roads are good" says Newcastle in 1750, "there come in here from Scotland every week by land carriage in Scotch carts very great quantities of Tobacco Stalks, which are carried from here in waggons all over the three [?] Southern Counties, and some to London, but we cannot prove their being run, tho' we imagine they must be, otherwise they could not afford to pay land carriage from two to four hundred miles upward."

1770. A.S. was now back in Kirkcaldy, dictating the *Wealth of Nations*; and Newcastle then reports:

"The tobacco trade without certificates, if allowed to go on, will put an end to many other fair dealers by underselling them. This tobacco comes from Whitehaven. . . . This strengthens our suspicions that in spite of the Restrictions of the Tobacco Act some considerable frauds are carried on in the Western Parts of the Island, the particular source of which it is not in our power to point out, whether by its being smuggled upon the Coast or by undue favor by the Discharging Officers upon the Quays or by Re-landing on exportation.

But we have been informed by a respectable dealer that he has had offers of tobacco to be sent from thence 30% below the current price, if he would run the risk of removal without Certificate—that considerable quantitys are sent from thence across the Island to the towns and villages upon the Border and even far into Northumberland and the country to the westward of it, so as greatly to prejudice him

[1] Noted in Scott, "Land and Water Carriage" (Glasgow University Library, reduced from folio). But I never located this folio.

and the fair traders in general—he points out the following method of Clandestine Conveyance of which he took some pains to be informed, in packages so as to resemble Bales or Trusses of Cloth etc. in parcels not exceeding 24 lbs. and if a larger quantity is to be sent to one person, it is divided into as many such parcels as are necessary, with a different direction on each, some to feigned names, others to persons in the place who are not dealers and are ignorant of the abuse made of their names, and all with some private mark by which the proper person may know and claim them and sometimes, when they remove by Certificate, by an expeditious management, it is made to serve a second time for a like quantity—all which we have thought it our duty to submit to your Honors."

But tobacco was not the only delinquent.

1783, Feb. Nicholas Armstrong, Riding Surveyor at Newcastle, reports the heavy smuggling of tea and spirits into the West Coast of Scotland by armed cutters:

> "600 ankers of spirits and 300 boxes of tea purchased by the smugglers at Langholm [on the Esk: Langholm Lodge was a seat of the Duke of Buccleuch] in Scotland, and the borders thereof, who have associated themselves into formidable bodies, and carry and convey these goods thro' the country into Cumberland, Northumberland and the South Countries, threatening the Riding Officer with murder."

(Another Armstrong, Robert by name, second mate of the *Eagle* Revenue Cutter, was equally zealous in complaints. Calling at the home of the Sunderland Collector, Ralph Lambton (February, 1774,) he was received to his chagrin with:

> "Damn you, you dirty scoundrel. What business have you at this Port, or to trouble me in this Place? This is not the place for Duty. You villain, get out of my sight."

There was plain speaking in those days.)

1783, April. Newcastle again reminds London:

> "We are not in the practice of *importing* tobacco at this *Port.*"

In 1783 the tobacco ports with warehousing privileges were London, Bristol, Liverpool, Cowes, Whitehaven, Greenock and Port Glasgow.

From the end of 1783 to March, 1801, Pitt was both Prime Minister and Chancellor of the Exchequer, and his masterful hand was soon at work.

1786, April.

> "Refce. yr Honors order concerning Frauds in the trade between Carlisle and Scotland, we answer:—
>
>   1.   350 hundred of tobacco were brought by certificate to manufacturers at Newcastle [last year]. . . .

4. Yr Honors have an Officer at Morpeth and at Hexham appointed for the sole purpose of preventing frauds in the Tobacco Trade.

5. We have no doubt that very great quantities of tobacco are smuggled on the West Coast of Scotland, the effects of which in some degree reach even to this place and neighbourhood, and have most probably a more powerful operation in those parts which are not guarded by officers of the Customs, and even where such officers are placed, the contrivances of the smugglers in disguising their packages, their chusing the night for the removal, and their evading the high roads where they suspect they are likely to be interrupted, and the opportunities affording by the various avenues to most provincial towns all concur to make it almost impossible to prevent smuggling of tobacco, especially when there is no check on the real stock of the dealers, and as the Excise Officers in the Inland Stations, we are inclined to suspect, pay very little attention to the Tobacco Trade, having perhaps full employment in their proper business of the Excise."

1786, July.

"Persons who receive from them the article called Shag [O.E.D. A strong tobacco cut into fine shreds, 1789[1]] sell it to the shopkeepers here even with a Certificate at such a price that they can retail it at 2d. a lb. less than is charged for the same article here wholesale by the manufacturers in London."

1789. Packages of tobacco must now, by law, be stamped TOBACCO.

"One in the trade says that the great source of fraud is the re-landing of tobacco exported for the Drawback, which ingenious trade has not only been carried on to a great extent on the West Coasts of England and Scotland, but has been practiced in the port of London, and that this finds its way back to some of the trade in packages, so as to pass as hops, bales of cloth etc. and there are some houses which greatly undersell the fair trader."

Down to 1789 the duty on tobacco, 1s. 3d. per lb. [what a trifle it seems to us of 1960!], was wholly levied as a Customs Import Duty. Pitt in 1790 left the duty at that rate, but levied 9d. of it as a duty of Excise and 6d. as a Customs duty, thus closing the administrative loophole reported by Newcastle in 1786.

Innocents at Home.

Chamber of Commerce Manifest, Glasgow, January 29, 1785:

"These are to certify that Messrs Aitken & Co of Glasgow have maintained an unblemished repute as fair traders and men of character:

[1] If you ask for shag today, they offer you a soft powdery tobacco.

that they have not been regular importers of tobacco and consequently are not well versed in the laws concerning that article: (the mistake) being in no respects the effect of design, but seems to have proceeded from inexperience alone."

Pat. Colquhoun   Chairman
Gilb. Hamilton   Secry.

The shipment had exceeded the amount shown on the Certificate by 182 lb.

Comment by Newcastle:

"We understand Mr. Colquhoun who styles himself Chairman of the Chamber of Commerce at Glasgow to be a gentleman of fair character and a considerable tobacco merchant. Of the Petitioner we know nothing."

Was he perhaps a forbear of the noble lord who left cement for politics and the press and coaxed us out of our aluminium utensils for aircraft construction in World War II?

Rather surprisingly there was also a coastal movement from South to North. In 1791 a York tobacconist, complaining of the insufficient time allowed by the Excise for transhipment, says he has to send to Montrose, Forfarshire, thus—by land to Stockton, by boat to Newcastle, and then by sea to Montrose, "being the only certain way of sending goods from hence to North Britain, there being no regular trade by sea."

Meet Mr. and Mrs. Simm.

March 3, 1733.

"The seizing officer at Newcastle reports: That the said Simm is a Scotchman and keeps an Alehouse frequently chiefly by Scotch farmers and masters of sloops that come from Scotland with corn etc. That the said Simm never buys any wine of merchants that import it nor has he a licence for selling wine. The wine seized was conceal'd in a garret, and when the officer seized the same, the said Simm could give but a very imperfect account of it. That at first he alleged it was his master's, who is a fitter in this town, afterwards his wife said it was a present to her, and neither of them pretended to say it had paid duty"—Honest fellow, and indeed "a person who, though no doubt highly blameable for violating the laws of his country, is frequently incapable of violating those of natural justice, and would have been, in every respect, an excellent citizen, had not the laws of his country made that a crime which nature never meant to be so." *W. of N.*, II, 381.

Adam Smith has much to say on highways, at home and abroad, in Europe and in Asia—but on highwaymen nothing. It would ill beseem a Southron to descant on the Scotland of Rob Roy, but who has not chuckled with W. R. Scott (*Adam Smith as Student and Professor*, 274) over the episode of Smith and the highwayman?—And if your man had shot, writes Wedderburn to him, October 30, 1777, "I shou'd have been in more pain for your danger than the highwayman's." Few were the travellers of his day who had not been called upon, once at least, to "stick 'em up." But sometimes the evil doers were brought to book.

Belfast News Letter of April 24, 1739.

"Last Saturday [April 7] Richard Turpin and John Stead were executed at Tyburn [York] for horse stealing. . . . Before his death he declared himself to be the notorious Highwayman Turpin and confessed a great number of robberies which he had committed."

> And the Bishop says, "Sure as eggs is eggs
> This here's the bold Turpin!"

The notice of the hero in the D.N.B. is written by a detractor—a descendant, perhaps, of "the mottle-faced gentleman." For an authentic account, with the available evidence, see *Immortal Turpin*, compiled by Arty Ash and written by Julius E. Day, Staples Press, 1948; and below, p. 93.

Adam Smith and Tobias Smollett.

In a passage familiar from the notoriety of the incident and the vigour of his language, Adam Smith adverts to tobacco:

"It was the object of the famous excise scheme of Sir Robert Walpole to establish, with regard to wine and tobacco, a system not very unlike that which is here proposed [public warehousing and no duty till taken out for home-consumption]. But though the bill which was then brought into parliament, comprehended those two commodities only; it was generally supposed to be meant as an introduction to a more extensive scheme of the same kind. Faction, combined with the interest of smuggling merchants, raised so violent, though so unjust, a clamour against that bill, that the minister thought proper to drop it; and from a dread of exciting a clamour of the same kind, none of his successors have dared to resume the project." (*Wealth of Nations*, II, 370.)

It was Pitt, who in his famous Warehousing Act of 1803 (43 Geo. 3 c. 134) brought the project into general force, conditionally upon the different ports meeting the requirements of the Act (Newcastle, July, 1804, had not yet qualified). As a West Indian merchant of the day said, "Best thing he ever did, the Union with Ireland excepted."[1]   But Adam Smith does not explain the system of bonding and drawback actually employed in his day for tobacco. Nor does he examine the nature of the all important re-export trade to France.   His citations concern the structure of the trade in the tobacco colonies (Virginia and Maryland, I, 346), the stimulus to Scottish banking (I, 280), and in chief (I, 454–6) the role of plantation produce in the Balance of Trade.   For enlightenment on the two further points, we must turn to business records, such as the Bogle Letters,[2] and of all things to that strange romance by Tobias Smollett (of whom more later in relation to the Press Gang), *Peregrine Pickle* of 1751.   In an inset (Chapter 98), which has as much relation to the general narrative as Gabriel Grub or the Queer Client to the Adventures of Sam Weller and Mr. Pickwick, Smollett gives us what is lacking in Adam Smith.

Mr. M–, his story goes, seeing

"with concern the great disadvantages under which our tobacco trade, the most considerable branch of our commerce with that people, was carried on; what inconsiderable returns were made to the planters out of the low price given by the French company,"

formed a plan to remedy the evil, and when the Excise Scheme miscarried, secured from the Ministry approval of his plan—but no action.   He, therefore,

"presented a plan to the French company, in which he set forth the advantages that would accrue to themselves from fixing the price, and securing that sort of tobacco which best suited the taste of the public and their manufacture."

The plan was accepted and he set off for Virginia to secure the concurrence of the planters, taking with him a little French abbé, who turns out to be the villain of the piece.   The planters readily assented,

"and the only difficulty that remained related to the security for the payment of the bills on the arrival of the tobacco in England, and to the time stipulated for the continuance of the contract."

To settle these points, he returned to Europe, leaving behind the abbé, who treacherously persuaded the planters that he could supply them at an easier rate, and the French company, that M–'s scheme would put them into his power, so that "they must afterwards submit to any price he should please to impose."

---

[1] Cf. *Huskisson and His Age*, 377.
[2] Cf. *Adam Smith and the Scotland of his Day*, 60.

In a dudgeon, M– refused to cooperate with "that little traitor," and told the French company that he would never enter into a scheme "that had a manifest tendency to lower the market price of tobacco in England!"   And Smollett, surely with his tongue in his cheek, concludes:

> "Thus ended a project in the execution of which M– had the good of the public, and the glory of putting in a flourishing condition the valuable branch of our trade, which gives employment to two great provinces and above two hundred sail of ships, much more at heart than his own private interest."

Smollettt and Smith were fellow Glaswegians.   I have always been hoping to find some interview or correspondence between them, but so far in vain.   Yet I can guess what Adam Smith thought when he read this piece of irony:

> "I have never known much good done by those who affected to trade for the public good.   It is an affectation, indeed, not very common among merchants, and very few words need be employed in dissuading them from it."   (I, 421.)

Chapter VI

COAL

NATURE OF COAL DUTIES—IRISH PRELUDE—CUSTOM HOUSE
BUSINESS—"FORCED OVERSEAS"—STOPS OF WORK—ROUNDABOUT
TRADE—CHANNEL ISLAND PRIVILEGES—IMPRESSMENT AND QUARAN-
TINE.

Coal: the fuel of commercial and industrial growth

Wealth of Nations, I, 351.

"The coal trade from Newcastle to London, for example, employs
more shipping than all the carrying trade of England, though the
ports are at no great distance."

Ibid., II, 358.

"If a bounty could in any case be reasonable, it might, perhaps, be
so upon the transportation of coals from those parts of the country
in which they abound, to those in which they are wanted. But the
legislature, instead of a bounty, has imposed a tax of three shillings
and three pence a ton upon coal carried coastwise, which upon most
sorts of coal is more than sixty per cent of the original price at the
coal-pit. Coals carried either by land or by inland navigation pay
no duty. Where they are naturally cheap they are consumed duty
free: where they are naturally dear, they are loaded with a heavy
duty."

The statistics, in the Newcastle Records, of ships belonging to
Newcastle illustrate the first point for the coastal trade as a whole:
e.g. in 1765:

> 51 ships, with tonnage of 7660, employing 459 men—foreign trade.
> 188 ships, with tonnage of 47,150, employing 2030 men—coastwise
> trade.

The Nature of the Coal Duties.

The coal duty was in principle an export duty, paid by the
shipper at the port of shipment. Its purpose was revenue. By the
end of the eighteenth century it was levied at different rates,
according as it was shipped coastwise within Great Britain; to
Ireland; to British Plantations; to foreign countries—with special
regulations for the Channel Islands. The principal market of Newcastle, the doyen of the trade, was London; of Swansea and Whitehaven, Ireland (the South of Ireland, and Dublin and the North of

Ireland, respectively).   The predominance of London in Newcastle's trade is further evidenced in the coal figures for 1791–99 (annual average):

To London: 357,000 chalders (1 Newcastle chalder = 53 cwt.).
,, other ports within Great Britain, 114,000 chalders.
,, foreign countries, 41,000 chalders.

Irish Prelude.

(Strafford Papers, Central Library, Sheffield, by courtesy of Earl Fitzwilliam and his trustees.)   Thomas Wentworth, Lord Deputy of Ireland to Sir William Raylton, his London man of business, July 17, 1635:

"In my dispatch to Mr. Secy Coke you will find my opinion touching the Imposition upon the Coals to the City of Dublin and those parts of this Kingdom which most use Coals.   Most insupportable.   Surely, if it should go on, it would put the whole trade of Colyery into the Scottish men's hands."   For Scotland had its own revenue system until the Union of 1707 by 6 Ann. c. 11.

To Mr. Secretary [John] Coke, May, 1635:

"You will receive a letter from this Council concerning the late imposition of five shillings upon a chaldron of all coals brought hither forth of England.   And I hold it my duty privately yet plainly to certify, that coals here all the year long are twice the price full that London is served for, but also in regard this Kingdom (being a member of England, and having with so universal a consent given so plentiful a supply, and passed so many beneficial laws for the Crown) should not be thought worthy of equal respect with other his Majesty's subjects, but be thus treated in their repute no otherwise as strangers and foreigners."

But by July, 1636, he was able to say:

"His Majesty's gracious favor to the People in taking off the 5 shilling the chaldron of coal I have made known unto them.   It is received with infinite acknowledgement and acclamation.   Howbeit indeed it was of necessity to be laid down and the commodity not being able to bear so heavy a charge, in so much as understanding, I wonder how it came to be thought upon.   Surely it was not well understood. For Ireland is served with coals forth of Scotland as well as forth of England and Wales—so as this imposition, not being laid in Scotland, they would have under sold both the other, and consequently have gained the whole trade of coals to themselves, which undoubtedly would have seen a great decay of shipping and trade between the two Kingdoms (one principal stay whereof is the Colliery) by means whereof his Majesty would have lost more presently in his custom, than the imposition would have come unto [cf. "The saying of Dr. Swift, that in the arithmetic of the customs two and two, instead of making four, sometimes make only one," *W. of N.*, II, 365], and in conclusion the Mines being by the owners forborne to be wrought as not profitable, even the imposition itself would have come to nothing too. Therefore I beseech you to hasten the directions to the Officers of the Customs that so the duty be not further demanded by them."

Well said, Mr. Thorow! And Scotland could at least thank him for speaking of "Scottish" men.

In and Around the Custom House.

By 1736, Newcastle's growing trade compelled them to ask for more commodious quarters.

"In it are at one end the several offices of the Collector, the Deputies Customers and Comptroller, which said offices wholly take up one end, and the other end is employed by the Duke of Richmond's Collector and Officers of the Coastal Coal Duty of 12d. per Chalder payable to his Grace, at each of which ends are garett lights, and no other light in the Custom House.[1]

In the middle of the house are placed the Land Surveyors and Tide Waiters offices on one side, the Tide Surveyors on the other side, which make the house very narrow. And the Land Surveyors and Land Waiters offices are so obscured from both the said Lights that it is with great difficulty they can see to write or make up any Books, and those of the Land Waiters containing 6 desks are so narrow, that they cannot pass or repass by each other, and the Land Waiters sitting at the end are obliged at all times to come out of their Offices to admit those who have the middle seats, which often retards their Business, and by the Noise and Hurry, when ships are to be cleared away, may subject them to mistakes in making up their books. There are also two late additional offices, one for an officer belonging to the Trinity House and another for the Corporation Officer, allowed by your Honors."

(Canadian students will visualise the impasse by thinking of the jam of cars outside their Science buildings; and tourists, like myself, of his host's difficulty in edging to a vacant space at the Airport.)

Therefore Newcastle asks for a

"Light and Convenient Room adjoining [i.e. for human parking space], which the proprietor is willing to let." Increase of rent only £15 p/a. "Otherwise it will be used by the owner, a wine merchant, to sell wine, coffee, etc., with a common staircase between it and the Custom House: which would be most inconvenient."

But very convenient to the idea of some ports in other days. Thus

[1] Charles II in 1677 granted to his natural son, the Duke of Richmond, and his heirs the duty of 1s. per chaldron on all sea coal shipped from Newcastle.

Yarmouth (and Mr. R. C. Jarvis several years ago sent us a delightful Christmas card, depicting the Custom House, Great Yarmouth, of the early eighteenth century—built for "the greatest herring merchant in Europe") writes to Lowestoft, 1708—in the reign of Queen Anne:

"Gentlemen,

Our good friend, our Queen's searcher, owning the Queen's Head in Lowestoft, a house of good entertainment and civil usage, as myself have experienced, and it being natural to help our friends and more particularly those of our own society, I suppose you will easily agree to my request, which is to desire you to promote the interests of the said house and cause all ships that are to be cleared and other Customs Business done in a Public House to be done there."

Your friend,
T.M.
Collector at Yarmouth.

Those were the days!

1766 is a landmark in Newcastle Customs history. For it saw the building of the new and present Custom House, which lies a little way below Tyne Bridge, the approximate site of the old house. The cellars, with groined brick ceilings which the craftsman of today could hardly equal, are being refitted as a Queen's warehouse—the room I saw contained many large *paper* bags of tobacco stalks—and leading down to them was a window with one pane of the original glass still there. It is fortunate, therefore, that we have the Collector's Letter, notifying the move.

"Hon Sirs,

We humbly acquaint you that the New Custom House not being in such readiness at Michaelmas, as was expected, we did not remove at that time nor did we think it altogether safe on account of the Damps which it was apprehended the walls might retain, but we then began to secure in the Cellars there such Liquors as were seized from that time, the warehouses in the Old Custom House being full, and as the removing the great quantity of Liquors there under Seizure, would have been attended with much Expence as well as an unavoidable waste, we judged it expedient to get them condemned, early in Term, and to sell them before we began to remove on the 22nd ultimo and on the 24th were virtually settled in the New Custom House. Mr. Pearetty undertaking to settle with Mr. Durham, the proprietor of the Old Custom House, his Rent for the Quarter and what more he might claim, on account of our not quitting the Premises at the time appointed, your Honors directions for payment of the Rents of the present Custom House are therefore humbly required.

We further acquaint your Honors that in the original Plan there were only two cellars designed, one of which is fill'd with several casks of Liquors taken up at different times floating at Sea, for the disposal whereof we have long attended the orders of the Admiralty, and the other is used as a Tackle House for lodging the Weights, Scales, Beams etc. used by the Waterside officers, no such place having been provided for—so that there remains only the two small vaults for the reception of seized liquors. Your Honors having disapproved of the use of the great vault in your letter of the 8th April last—But on the late occasion of the Securing Forty Five Casks of Spirits and Wine, which we represented to you, we found it necessary to make use of the said vault by means of a small communication or opening between it and the smaller ones which was left for Air. We flatter ourselves your Honors will not disapprove of what has been done and will also consent that the original intended entrance into the vault may be broke open without which the Casks in question cannot without great difficulty and hazard be got up again. We further acquaint your Honors that the Duke of Richmond's Receiver, who has an office in the long Room, has his Grace's arms carved and finished in a very elegant manner placed over him and there being no painting of the King's Arms except a very old one which has usually been placed in the Patent Board, but is now unfit to be affixed, in this new office, it is humbly submitted whether it would not be proper to have a New Coat of His Majesty's Arms prepared and put up over the Collector.

We are etc.

L. S.   R. P.

24th January, 1767.

P.S. We pray to know whether your Honors will please to allow the expense of covering the Desks with Green Cloth which is necessary to be done, they being only made of Fir."

The interior of a Custom House has, perhaps, as much to tell the economic historian as a Blenheim or a Holkham, yet when talking coal, we must except one great building, the ornate edifice which houses the Bowes Museum near Barnard Castle, County Durham (the Wallace cum South Kensington Collection of the North); for it was built on coal, and a Customs entry of 1766 introduces Mrs. George Bowes, the mother of the lady who became Mary Eleanor Bowes Lyon, Countess of Strathmore, the "Unhappy Countess" of Ralph Arnold's biography, and the great grandmother of the John Bowes who in 1869 founded the Bowes Museum. (Incidentally, the first screw collier, built to the design of C. M. Palmer of Jarrow, was named the *John Bowes*.) The entry reads:

"There is come coastwise to this port from London without any Coast Dispatch 51 Trunks, Boxes and Parcels of Goods directed to Mrs.

Bowes of Gibside, and among them a Chest containing 33 lbs of tea, 6 lbs of coffee, and 6 of chocolate, accompanied with a Permit. No fraud intended (for we are convinced the goods do really belong to Mrs. Bowes), yet it may be of bad consequence to the Revenue to suffer such quantities of valuable goods to be shipt without the presence of an officer and unaccompanied by proper dispatches, and may give opportunities for designing persons to carry on frauds by falsely addressing their goods to persons of distinction."

Gibside, near Gateshead in North Durham, with the coal seams which run beneath its policies, as seen on Friday, January 16, 1959, after a week of high wind and icy snow, might have been somewhere in Mining Ontario. Approached from above one saw the huge stone column, appearing against a background of blue sky as tall as London's Monument, with the figure of Liberty on top, and beyond it the mile-long terrace with its avenues of leafless trees glittering with frosted snow; the Georgian stable block; the fruit garden surrounded by a 12 foot wall of red brick; the remnants of the mausoleum with the crypt out of which small shrubs sprouted; and finally the great house itself, now in ruins—the original mansion in graceful Jacobean with W.B., April 12, 1620 on the portal, and the larger block added by George Bowes over a century later. The house faces south, but the grand view is from the great dining room, looking north across the Derwent to Rowland's Gill. W.B. stands for William Blakiston, the last Blakiston baronet of Gibside, whose property passed by marriage in 1691 to the Sir William Bowes who helped his neighbour Ambrose Crowley of Winlaton to establish the iron works at Blaydon and thereabouts. But it was George Bowes with James Paine as architect who made Gibside one of the stately homes of Northern England.

John Bowes, 1811–85, the great grandson of George, was a notable Victorian, four times winner of the Derby, with a famous racing stud at Streatham Castle, South Durham. The friend of Thackeray (he comes into *Barry Lyndon*) at Cambridge and Paris; the step-son of William Hutt, M.P. for Gateshead, who carried on Huskisson's imperialism; he married in Paris the French actress Mlle Delorme, and the two assembled the great collection which was removed to England and given Public Museum status by Parliament in 1871. On the way back from Rowland's Gill over Scotswood Bridge to Newcastle I noticed waggons marked J. Bowes, N.C.B. (National Coal Board).

Harwich, with its stream of gentlefolk bringing back souvenirs of the Grand Tour, knew more about the "slipping in" racket than any other port—leather bags concealed at the back part within the breeches (like the old clergyman who is said to have abstracted thus the Cambridge Modern History volume by volume, till the final volume of maps caught in the turnstile), as well by gentlemen, as by their servants; and ladies protected by the privilege of their sex.

"When the tide surveyor found she had something concealed in her stays, she took him round the neck and held and kissed him a considerable time. And when Mr. O and Mr. P (senior officers) went to her to the public house and acquainted her they had an information that she had some prohibited goods about her, she immediately lifted her petticoats to her waist. . . ."

But modesty forbids.

The Clearing of Coals, Coastwise and Oversea.

Report of December, 1753, to Mr. Secretary Woods:

"Coals are brought from Pits in Waggons and laid on Staiths erected by the River Side and from these cast into Keels or Lighters, measured by the Commissioners appointed thereto generally to 8 chaldrons, weighing 53 cwt. to the chalder, and carried down the River in those Keels and delivered on board the Ships. And no ship is cleared coastwise until a certificate of the quantity she has is obtained from the Duke of Richmond's Collector of the 12d. per chalder, and we have reason to believe his Grace's officers are very exact in ascertaining the quantity of coals each vessel takes on, not only the first but for several succeeding voyages till they are fully satisfied what every vessel employed in the Coast trade is capable of taking in, and there are innumerable instances of ships that have been charged with [sc. charged for duty on] a greater quantity of coals than what they took in their first voyage, for it's the practice of the Duke's officer to observe what depth of water every vessel draws when loaden with coals the 1st voyage as well as the number of chaldrons she takes in, and in future voyages they privately inspect the same again, and raise them to a higher quantity according as they are loaded, and when any of these vessels have afterwards been entered for oversea and strictly watched by a Tidesman on board they have not at any time been found to take in more coals than what the Duke of Richmond's officers have charged them with in their Coast voyage.

When a ship is outward bound with Coals the Master or his Agent takes out a Sufferance for a certain quantity, for which he deposits the duty till the ship is laden, it being often uncertain what quantity she can take in, which Sufferance is delivered to the Tide Surveyor, who places a Tidesman on board to keep an account on the back thereof of the number of chalders received on board. During the time the ship is loading the Tidesman is frequently visited by the Tide Surveyor who, when the ship is loaded, certifies the Builth of the Ship on the Sufferance and incloses the same directed to the Collector and

Surveyor, the Surveyor examines and certifies the particulars, for which perfect Entries and Coquets are then made out, and if the whole quantity of Coals was not taken, the Duty is returned."

Thus Parkinson's Law is already at work in an eighteenth century garb.

Newcastle, unlike Swansea, took no interest in Culm:

November, 1776.

"We humbly report [this is a customary signal of contempt] that there is no such article as Culm shipt at this Port. . . . Culm is, as we are informed, the small, or refuse of Welch coals. An attempt was made to ship small coals at a Creek of this Port as Culm, but a sample of it was reported by the Coal Meters of London to be very different from Culm."

They never knew any small coals coming from the North to be entered as Culm. The tone is that of the first Directors of the Liverpool and Manchester Railway—"they'll be asking us to carry 3rd class passengers next!"

1777.

"About 4000 ships load here coastwise in the year and sometimes it happens that a hundred ships or more are loading at one and the same time in different parts of the River, and there is no way to ascertain the quantity of coals actually put on board on every repeated voyage but by the means of an officer every time. In the present mode of transacting it, viz. by fixing each vessel at the highest rate, the mistake seldom can happen but on the right side, which was the case with the *Sally* above mentioned, which was rated at 32 Chas. but on the voyage in question only took 30 Chas."

1795.

"Coals being shipt here by the Newcastle chalder from Keels containing a certain number of chaldrons denoted by nails or marks there [like the Plimsoll load-line of our day], it has been the practice of ancient standing to estimate a keel of 8 chalders Newcastle at 15 Winchester measure. This proportion, however, cannot be exact nor can there be any certain agreement between weight and measure [Swansea with its hard anthracite measured by 'heap,' other export centres by 'strike,' as in the grain trade]: because coals of different mines differ in their specific gravities, because they are sometimes delivered round and at other times small, and because the keels are sometimes and particularly in the winter made heavy by continued rains, so that they are brought down to their marks by a less weight than in the dry weather and consequently will appear to have in more coals than they actually have and these circumstances contribute to that uncertainty by the bushel or vat which appears in the making out Coastwise of the proportion above mentioned being sometimes exceeded . . . while at other ports less."

For simplicity of calculation Newcastle suggests that, if and when the oversea duty is raised, 1 Newcastle chaldron be reckoned as 2 Winchester with a consequent slight gain to the Revenue.

In actual fact, in 1800 the rates in Winchester chaldrons, omitting fractions, were:

Coastwise	..	5s. 9d. (reached by increments over the century)[1]
Into London		9s. 3d. (where there was a heavy City duty of old standing)

Exported

To Ireland ..	..	..	..	..	..	..	1s. 3d.
To British Plantations in America	..	..	..	2s. 5d.
To Other Places in British ships	..	..	..	£1 2s. 0d.
in Foreign ships	..	..	..	£1 15s. 3d.

([C 8706] Customs Tariffs of the United Kingdom, p. 59.)

The Fiction of "Forced Overseas."

1736, March. "Received £23 2. 0. for oversea duty of 77 chaldrons of coals, Newcastle measure, ship't for Lynn but delivered at Sheedam [Schiedam, W. of Rotterdam]: forced oversea before the duty was paid."

1749, March. *Re* ships clearing coastwise but delivering in foreign ports:—

Sunderland (fitters and merchants) desire a stiffening of the regulations, but Newcastle says it is best to carry on as at present, in order not to hold up trade—viz. Collector to accept of the Oversea Duty from the Masters [of ships] on Affidavit made of their being *forced* oversea. Customs, be it noted, had a hold on the shippers, as is evidenced by the "Accounts of Bonds taken for coals which have been entered coastwise and have been carried overseas, and to which Process has been sent from the Exchequer, but as yet the duties for such coals remain unpaid."

Specimen entry:—

Date of Bond	Where given	Bonds-men	Ship and Master	Chas. of Coals	Penalty of Bonds	Amount of duties
March 3, 1749	New-castle	J.V. R.W. J.B.	*True Briton*	207	£207	£62.2.0.

[1] = 4s. 3d. per ton, as compared with Adam Smith's 3s. 3d.—above p. 56.

1756. Newcastle, after a visit to Sunderland, reports to London:

"All or most of the Masters who clear'd and deliver oversea do it voluntarily for the following reasons, viz. it is well known that such masters agree with their men for an Oversea Voyage, that they keep company on their passage with Masters bound for London etc. as far as Cromer etc. when they leave the English coast and proceed abroad, whilst the others continue their voyages and deliver coastwise—also want of Money to pay the Oversea Duty before they go I find to be the reason among many of them, so that it's generally believed not four ships in any year out of the number that are sworn to be forced oversea are actually so, and that several of their Masters have been heard to say that they never regard any part of the Affidavit they swore to except that Part that they had no intention of Fraud."

August, 1956. Figures for Newcastle, 1748–55 (aggregate or average?):

Coals "forced oversea" c, 3,000 chalders
  entered for oversea c, 20,000   ,, } roughly 1 to 7.

It was thus at Newcastle still the exception rather than the rule.

1773.

"The quantities of Spirits, Tea and other prohibited goods continually moving by land from Sunderland to Gateshead, Durham, and to various parts of the County plainly prove it [sc. the slackness of Sunderland Customs]: and in the Coal Trade the greatest part of the vessels which clear coastwise at Sunderland with coals and pretend to be forced overseas to Holland etc. from whence they generally return in ballast (and the exportation of coals to foreign parts is chiefly carried on in this manner) could not be supported by the fair profits of the voyage, but the Masters call in smuggling to their aid to enable them to make a living."

As Canning might have phrased it, "calling in a New Trade to redress the balance against the Old."

And the crews, too, were advantaged in their pays. An owner told Newcastle (1786) that:

"it was the custom of Sunderland to pay the people's wages at the port oversea and that they laid the amount out on such articles as might make their voyage more advantageous to them at their arrival home."

Over now to Sunderland, where the fiction by 1760 was the established rule, condoned by the Commissioners of Customs.

1761. London to Sunderland:

"If overseas Duties are deposited as alleged, bring them to account."

Then follow lists for the past year of "forced overseas" ships which cleared from Sunderland and had reported to London, five lists in all—28, 19, 19, 14, 23. Year by year the lists continue at increasing length; and as the names of the ships are given, these often occupy the larger part of the instructions from London.

1762. A ship, "forced overseas," gets a new mainsail at Rotterdam, falsely stamped as "duty paid." Therefore ship is seized on her return, and surveyor refuses to accept the duty offered.

1707. In a lawsuit "Benj. Hodgskin is allowed by the Commissioners £16 for getting the Overseas duty from coastwise coals over a period of years—£189 in all, as his services do not come within the Costs paid by Defendant."

1707. London to Sunderland, re the necessity of full returns for statistical purposes, of the "forced oversea" business.

"Unless you do insert such vessels which return to your Port after having been forced oversea with coals, though they do not amount to one fifth part of the real muster which were forced oversea within the quarter, it will be impossible for the Registrar General of Shipping to render an Acct. of the Foreign an Coast Trade in the Kingdom. I find from the objections you have stated that it is necessary to inform you that the impropriety which you apprehend would be the consequence of your inserting so small a part of the ships or vessels forced oversea, as almost to be totally reconciled by a List which the Registrar General requires from the several Collectors, of such ships which come into their Ports and pay the Duties on Coals on their return to England from being forced oversea, and the List furnished him with the Quantities of Coals for which Overseas Duties are received, as also the Port from whence such ships cleared coastwise, enables us, with some care and pains, in marking off against the respective ports, to ascertain pretty nearly a true Acct. of the Voyages Foreign and Coastwise. Scarboro generally sends a long list of ships, under this circumstance, and they are generally such as cleared coastwise at your Port or Newcastle."

The forced oversea lists for 1775 contain in one case c. 150 ships in another c. 200!

But it might work the other way round—ships that had paid the oversea duty genuinely compelled by stress of weather to deliver their cargo coastwise. Thus in 1787 we find 102 signatures to a Petition of Sunderland Shipowners stating that

"the ships that clear for foreign parts with coals and afterwards by contrary winds etc. are obliged to deliver cargoes coastwise, when they pay the coast duty, and when they return, cannot have the Overseas Duties repaid, until your Honors are petitioned, which takes time, and prevents ships from going foreign for want of money to pay a

second duty, besides putting many of them to the greatest inconven-
ience to pay the Fitters for their Coals and other expenses."

They ask, therefore, for repayment of the Foreign Duty by the
Collector at Sunderland, upon certificate of the Coast Duties having
been paid for the identical cargo.

One would like to hear Jeremy Bentham on this Fiction of the
Sea.

Imitation, they say, is the sincerest form of flattery.   In the Social
and Economic Survey of Swansea and District, Pamphlet 4, "The
Economic Development of Swansea and of the Swansea District to
1921" (1940) by D. Trevor Williams we read, p. 23:

> "The usual methods of the masters and merchants to evade taxation
> were to enter cargoes for home ports and then take their ships to
> Irish or continental ports, and, if discovered, to give their reasons as
> stress of weather, a favourable convoy, or a better market for coal in
> Ireland or on the continent."

The writer is commenting on the seventeenth century trade;
therefore a memorandum of 1782 by Swansea Customs on "How to
stop coals cleared coastwise from going oversea" does but tell an
old old story.   As with Sunderland and the North Sea, so with
Swansea and St. George's Channel—by the 1760's it was almost
routine for a ship cleared for Bideford or Falmouth to be driven by
contrary winds to Waterford or Cork.   Which was imitating which?
Or must we class it under the familiar heading "nothing new under
the sun," and ascribe it to the Parent of Lies?

The Keelmen and "Stops" of Work.

Wealth of Nations, I, 68–9.

> "We rarely hear, it has been said, of the combinations of masters;
> though frequently of those of workmen.   But whoever imagines,
> upon this account, that masters rarely combine, is as ignorant of the
> world as of the subject.   Masters are always and everywhere in a
> sort of tacit, but constant and uniform combination, not to raise the
> wages of labour above their actual rate. . . . We seldom, indeed,
> hear of this combination, because it is the usual, and one may say the
> natural state of things which nobody ever hears of. . . . Such
> combinations, however, are frequently resisted by a contrary and
> defensive combination of the workmen; . . . They are desperate,
> and act with the folly and extravagance of desperate men, . . . The
> masters upon these occasions . . . never cease to call aloud for the
> assistance of the civil magistrate, and the rigorous execution of those
> laws which have been enacted with so much severity against the
> combinations of servants, labourers and journeymen."

E.g. (as in Cannan's footnote 2 on p. 68) the laws against London
tailors, woolcombers and weavers, and tile and brick makers within
15 miles of London.[1]

The keelmen, be it remembered, were themselves little masters,
like the handloom weavers of the nineteenth century.

1738, April.   Newcastle to London.   Report on the State of the
Coal Trade.   This report was prompted by the complaint of the
masters of ships from Whitby, Scarbro' and Sunderland, who had
come to Newcastle to get supplies of coal, in order to circumvent the
new imposition of London Coal Buyers by Limitation of Vend, with
consequent restriction of shipments.   The fitters, says Newcastle,
are not in *formal* correspondence with ship owners, "neither can we
discover combination among the coal owners"; and the Report
concludes:

> "The Coal owners of this place do not appear to sell their coals to the
> Masters, the whole matter being transacted betwixt the Hostmen
> (generally call'd Fitters) and the Masters, for these Fitters are a
> company and have a right to ship Coals, so that the Custom or Method
> is that each Fitter agrees with his respective coal owner at every
> Christmas for his yearly Quantity, which is led to his particular place
> or Keel berths on the Staith, and from thence are taken away as the
> Fitter has occasion, and the Fitter pays the [coal] owner, so that in
> the whole the Coal trade is carried on in this River betwixt the
> Fitter and the Master of the Ship."

1738, May 2.

> "The Keelmen (who convey the Coals from the Staith to the Ship)
> having found a decay in their business by the late method of delivering
> in turn at London, between three and four hundred of the said Keel-
> men (as we are informed) assembled together this day and stopt every
> keel upon the River from delivering their coals into any ships either
> for overseas or coastwise, so that at present an entire stop is put to the
> Coal trade by the said Keelmen.   We believe the Civil Magistrates
> will scarce be able to quiet these people and get them to work again,
> without a military assistance, tho' they are now endeavouring to
> effect it."

May 6.

> "The Magistrates and Fitters have had several conferences with the
> said Keelmen but without any success, their demands (as we are
> informed) being so unreasonable that they cannot be comply'd with.
> We are humbly of opinion that this Stop in the Coal trade will be

[1] For the early benefit and union clubs of Swansea and district, see *Industrial Relations* (Pamphlet No. 4 in the University College of Swansea series)
by P. S. Thomas, M.A., 1940.

continued till some other Methods are taken with these men that obstruct it."

May 12.

"On Wednesday last in the afternoon the Keelmen went to work again so that the Coal trade here is under the same footing as it was before."

1738–39. *A Coalowner's Stop.*

Friction at Blyth between the authorities and the Ridleys, the great coal-owning family (which was represented in the nineteenth century by the statesman Sir Matthew White Ridley, who *inter alia* developed the town of Blyth).

Ridleys stop loading in protest against the new regulations for the marking of waggons.

"Mr. Ridley orders his waggon way to be repaired, so that no waggons can come down that way."

The Stewards of the Hostmen's Company and the Hostmen's Company and the other Fitters and persons concerned in the coal trade

"are very unwilling to be put out of their old way of admeasurement."

And who, they ask, is to pay for the brass plates prescribed by the Act?

1750, March.

"It is believed that for some time past there hath been an agreement among several of the Coal owners which it's now said is broke, and in order to rival each other in trade several of their agents endeavoured to make the Keelmen put more coals into their Keels (for the Coast) than they were admeasured to carry, which hath occasioned the whole body of Keelmen consisting of about 1500 to assemble together and stop working, nor will they allow any Keels to ply upon the River even to carry goods to and from ships. The Magistrates had sent them word they were in Court and ready to hear any complaints they had to make but they have not yet appear'd before them, tho' [the magistrates] have had a meeting with the Fitters, who say that their stopping work on acct. of desiring them to carry more coals than Measure is only a pretence, for that they have drawn up a list of Particular Indulgencies that cannot be granted them. There are now here 3 Companys of Lord A'-s soldiers, and we hear more is sent for, so how this will end is uncertain."

1775. Customs had seized three keels for discrepancies between quantity of coal reported and quantity actually shipped thence.

1775, February.   John Calhoun, the Crown's evidence for these Seizures,

"being suspected to be the informer has been dismissed from his employment as a Keelman by Messrs. Mosley and Airey, his former employer, and being refused to be hired by other fitters on the same acc^t., by which he finds himself distressed, notwithstanding his subsistence at a shilling a day (that being very short of the wages which keelmen may earn), we humbly desire that he may be entered as a Mariner on board the new [Revenue] shallop fitting out for Capt. Armstrong.   He is a stout able young man, has been brought up on the water and has served on board a King's ship."

And who is on the law's side?

1786, August 28.

"Last week the Keelmen employ'd in carrying coals from some of the Collieries in this River thinking themselves aggrieved by over measure made a stop, refusing to conduct their keels to the ships, and stopt also the other keels that were not suspected to be overladen, on which the Coal owners and Fitters, having met, as we understand, agreed to give orders to their Staithmen not to suffer any more than the just measure to be put into the keels, which satisfied the Keelmen and they returned to their work. . . .

On the whole, as the Keelmen seldom complain without reason, we thought proper to give an order to the Tide Surveyors [enclosed]. In some years it has been the practice of the Coal Owners to enter into an agreement by which the quantity to be vended by each in the year was fixed, of late one person has stood out[1] and they [the one concern] being at liberty to sell as much as they can, there is a competition, and we suppose that overmeasure is given to help the sale, and not with intention to defraud the Revenue, as they know that keels for ships oversea come more immediately under the inspection of the Officer of the Customs, and greater exactness is observed with respect to their loadings, and we understand the overmeasure to be in the Coast trade."

Mutinous Seamen.

1789, March.

"There has been within our observation several insurrections of the seamen in this port [Newcastle], in order to extort an increase of wages or to compel a redress of some grievances, real or imaginary, in which they have not only refused to go to sea in the ships they were hired to, but have forced from their ships such seamen as were

---

[1] George Bowes, M.P., who died in 1760, "embarked on a one-man policy of price-cutting, to the despair of his partners but to his own very considerable profit" (*Unhappy Countess*, 15).   In 1790 the eldest son of the Countess, John, 10th Earl of Strathmore, came of age.   Were the Trustees of the Bowes estates in Durham following in the 1780's the lead of the deceased George Bowes, or is it some other concern?

better disposed and have sometimes proceeded to unrigg the ship and have threatened more alarming outrages, and they have generally effected their purpose, whether thro' want of sufficient energy in the laws or resolution in the execution of them we do not presume to say; but we find that the 2 George 2 [c. 36], which makes mariners liable to punishment for refusing to go to sea, does not apply to the Coal or Coasting Trade, the principal trade of this great port"—

presaging the famous mutinies of 1797 in the Royal Navy at Spithead and the Nore.

It was in the prolonged voyages of the roundabout trade that difficulties over recruitment and wages were most likely to arise. Thus, the Petition of John Renwick, Master and part owner of the snow *Atlanta*, August 20, 1787, sheweth

"that in Septr. 1785 he sailed from Newcastle to the Baltic, the whole crew British, where he took a freight for Barcelona and from thence continued going from one Foreign Port to another until his arrival at Bremen 24 April last, from which place he sailed in ballast to Memel and then took in a full cargo of Timber to this Port [Newcastle,] arriving 27 July.

That the Officers of the Customs here have charged him with the Alien Duty on the said Timber because 6 men out of the 14 he had on board were foreigners, which nothing but absolute necessity alone obliged him to employ in the course of 2 years absence from England, and he was forced to leave one man ill at Elsinore, so that there was no other alternative, he hath since discharged all the foreigners and sent them home again according to the agreement made when engaged."

Again, the Petition of Charles Peace, Commander of the ship *Polly* of Poole in the County of Dorsetshire, 1791, sheweth

"That yr petitioner sailed from Poole about 3 months ago, from thence to Naples, from thence to Gallipoli and to return from thence to Amsterdam and lately arrived at Newcastle for the purpose of taking in a cargo of coals for Poole.

That having agreed with his sailors previous to his leaving England to pay them after the rate of 30s. a month if Peace continued or 40s. a month in the case of War [over Nootka Sound], a dispute arose at the said Port of Newcastle as to such payment between yr Petitioner and his Crew, whereupon the said crew, in revenge that the said Petitioner had not paid them according to their demand, laid an information against yr Petitioner having contraband goods aboard the said ship, altho' the proper officer belonging to the said Port had been discharged from the said ship, after having performed his duty, 8 days before the laying of such information. . . ."
the release of ship and cargo, seized in consequence thereof, is humbly prayed.

30s. and 40s. recalls the *Wealth of Nations*, I, 117.

"In time of war, when forty or fifty thousand sailors are forced from the merchant service into that of the king, the demand for sailors to merchant ships necessarily rises with their scarcity, and their wages upon such occasions commonly rise from a guinea and seven-and-twenty shillings, to forty shillings and three pounds a month."

Adam Smith would be thinking of the wars of 1741–48 and 1756–63. But over the *Polly* he would have shed no tear; for he rated but low the roundabout foreign trade.

"Roundabout foreign trade of consumption" is Adam Smith's pet phrase, e.g. I, 348–9 and I, 455, where he appears to have the Atlantic trade pattern in mind. The near-by pick-up trade in the form of coals to Denmark and in return timber from Norway was natural and economical, and Newcastle in 1801 emphasised the large trade from Hull to Newcastle in Baltic produce. But the necessarily longer Mediterranean trade, where ships cleared with coal or grain for the Levant and returned with oil, fruits and wine, picked up in return, was equally natural and economical. The "roundabout foreign trade of consumption" was only an extension of this: and his low rating of it is very unconvincing.

He argues:

"The returns of the foreign trade of consumption seldom come in before the end of the year, and sometimes not till after two or three years. A capital, therefore, employed in the home-trade will sometimes make twelve operations, or be sent out and returnes twelve times, before a capital employed in the foreign trade of consumption has made one. If the capitals are equal, therefore, the one will give four and twenty times more encouragement and support to the industry of the country than the other." (I, 348.)

To which Cannan appends the severe footnote:

' If this doctrine as to the advantage of quick returns had been applied earlier in the Chapter [i.e. Book II Chapter V of the Different Employment of Capitals], it would have made havoc of the argument as to the superiority of agriculture [on I.346].

We call to mind something more fundamental. For us the *Atlanta* and the *Polly* are typical "tramps," which O.E.D. defines as "a cargo vessel, which takes cargoes wherever obtainable and for any port." In 1914 "tramp steamers" (widely defined) accounted for 60 per cent of the steamship tonnage of the British Empire—a valuable mass of fluid transportation moving freely around the world, and altogether beneficial to the country which owned it.

The Privileges of the Channel Islands.

Wealth of Nations, II, 119.

"The islands of Guernsey and Jersey, without any means of resisting the authority of parliament, are more lightly taxed than any part of Great Britain."

The fiscal autonomy of the Channel Islands, resting on ancient right, and never seriously challenged, was accompanied by a privileged status in other fields—exemption from the operations of the Press Gang; an allowance of wool, the export of which was otherwise prohibited, for their stocking industry; free entry of their corn into the English market; and exemption from the oversea duty on coal. The last is a complicated story, and as with the other privileges, the abuse of it was restrained. Entries in the Customs Records of Swansea and Newcastle illustrate the position.

Swansea.

1766, July.

"The act made last session Cap XL for allowing the exportation of a certain quantity of coals free of the said duty to the Isles of Jersey, Guernsey and Alderney shall be punctually observed by us."

1770. A Jersey master with Coals for France "bound unto Mr. Thos. Haskar, Principal Officer of the Customs in that Island in the sum of £15," seeks permission to export the same from Jersey on paying the Export Duty.

London to Sunderland.

1778, July.

"It has been represented that the works ordered for the defence of Jersey and Guernsey cannot be executed while the present embargo between England and those islands remains: it is therefore ordered that the embargo be taken off all ships from Gt. Britain to Jersey and Guernsey with lime, bricks, timber etc. necessary for the said works on condition that the said ships do not carry more seamen than are absolutely necessary for their navigation."

(Stephen Cottrell for Privy Council.)

November—A similar order for Alderney.

Newcastle.

1784. *Re* coal for Jersey with licence from the Lieutenant Governor:

"Messrs. Mosley and Airey are informed that the whole quantity allowed by law was done except 90 chaldrons and that for all above that the full *oversea* duty must be paid: which we have accordingly deposited, but beg leave to observe on behalf of the Garrison and Inhabitants of Jersey that we believe there was an Order in Council to allow an additional 500 chas. to be ship't without paying the Oversea Duty."

Swansea.

1785.

"The exports from Neath are coals and copper, which are carried coastwise to Ireland, Man and the Islands of Guernsey and Jersey."

February 11, 1785. The Brig *Patty* from Neath for Guernsey, laden with coals, puts into Swansea in distress:

"Having reason to suspect that a very fraudulent trade is carried on in the exportation of coals from Wales to Guernsey and Jersey,"

Swansea asks for cooperation from other ports to ensure that the proper Duties (on export) may be paid: and thinks that the language of the Act should be amended.

Newcastle.

1788. John Champion, Register at Guernsey, to John Gale, Esq., Secretary of Customs, London (the Register was a British officer, and his presence was welcome because only by due Registration of their Shipping could the Channel Islands enter the charmed circle of Colonial trade).

"One thing is still done which I have lately discovered, that by the Act of 17 Dec. 1765 the Inhabitants of Guernsey, Jersey and Alderney are allowed a certain quantity of coals to be exported for the consumption of these Islands duty free, several vessels belonging to this Island are constantly employed in carrying coals from Newcastle and Swanzey, they come into the Road loaded, and the next tide proceed to France with their cargoes. . . ."

Newcastle comments:

"As the Act of the 6 Geo. 3 allowing the exportation from this Port of certain quantities of coal to Jersey, Guernsey and Alderney, free of the duty imposed by an Act of the 5th year on condition that the certificates therein mentioned under the Hands and Seals of the respective Governors of those Islands be produced to us, it has not been the practice to take any security for the due landing such coals at the Islands for which cleared. . . ."

Swansea.

1789.

"Yr Petitioner sailed from Swanzey in the Brig *Young Mary*, of and bound to the Island of Jersey, with a cargo of coals, for which coals he paid foreign duties of 15s. and 5d. per chaldron Newcastle measure"; and in bad weather had to heave some of his coal over-board, after which driven by contrary winds he put back into this Port and being in want of supplies for his vessel he made application to the Customs here to sell his coals.   If he can sell his coals locally, can he recover the duty over and above the coastwise rate?

Swansea.

1793.   To Collector of Customs, Swansea:

"Guernsey 29 June 1793 [England being now at War with France] Sir, I find that the Brig *Providence* Stephen Read Master, is now in the Port of Swansea ready to be loaded with coals for this Island, I beg to inform you that the description of coals called the Jones and Newbank Landor is much wanted in this Island for the Brickmakers and Blacksmiths of the King's Works, and that it will be for the convenience of this Island and for the good of His Majesty's service that the Brig before mentioned should be loaded and cleared out for Guernsey—

The late Lt. Governor, my predecessor, did grant a Permit for this Brig to load coal.

I am, etc.,

Thomas Dundas,

Lt. Govr. of Guernsey."

August, 1793.

"Yr Petitioner, George Walker of His Majesty's Island of Guernsey, having obtained a licence from the Lt. Govr. of Guernsey to import to Guernsey x chaldrons of coal [figure indistinct] for his own use in this Island free of the oversea duty, he sent the Licence, with a letter from the Lt. Govr. to Swansea Customs, who peremptorily refused to clear him," thus obliging him to pay the oversea duty "contrary to the privileges which His Majesty and His Royal Predecessors have been pleased to grant to the Inhabitants of this Island."

So, putting into Falmouth he paid the duty of £7 5s. 9d., and now asks for the return of it.   (Dundas backs the Petition, saying that "he was obliged to pay the Oversea Duty, altho' it is expressly provided by Act of Parliament that Coals from Newcastle and Swanzey should come duty free"—a bald statement, clearly requir-ing qualification.) Swansea explains that under the General Embargo in force at the time, they could not clear him, as he was neither armed nor intended to sail in convoy—thus shifting the issue.

As with the exemption from impressment, which like impressment itself had no *statutory* foundation, so with the enactments relating to wool, coal and corn, the whole story must be viewed in the light of the unswerving attachment of the Channel Islands to the British

Crown from William of Normandy onwards. Altogether different was the atmosphere in which the century closed with respect to "unhappy Ireland," when Swansea (March, 1798) was warned to be on the look-out for "Lord Edward Fitzgerald and other accomplices suspected of High Treason," and announced (July, 1799):

> "Safely arrived the property of George Bland, lately residing near Wexford, who last year having, by the providential relief of that place from the rebels by His Majesty's troops, been rescued from impending death, and being warned of the danger he was in by assassination, in revenge for the testimony given by him at the trial of several of the chief rebels, prays exemption from duties for the furniture saved from the plunder of his house."

We are not given the answer of Hon. Sirs. But doubtless they said "yes," remembering, perhaps, Kilcoman Castle and the author of the *Fairie Queene*.

The Press for Seamen.

Not Adam Smith, but Tobias Smollett, his near contemporary at Glasgow University, supplies the texts here, and both are classic.

> (i) "As I crossed Tower-wharf, a squat tawny fellow, with a hanger by his side, and a cudgel in his hand, came to me, calling, 'Yo, ho! brother, you must come along with me.' . . . After an obstinate engagement . . . I was disarmed, taken prisoner and carried on board a pressing tender: where, after being pinioned like a malefactor, I was thrust down into the hold, among a parcel of miserable wretches, the sight of whom well nigh distracted me."—*Roderick Random*, Ch. 24.
>
> (ii) "Dear Sir
> I am again your petitioner in behalf of that Great Cham of literature, Samuel Johnson. His black servant, whose name is Francis Barber, has been pressed on board the *Stag* frigate, Captain Angel, and our lexicographer is in great distress."

Tobias Smollett to John Wilkes, Chelsea, March 16, 1759.

1746, July. Admiralty to Philip Saumarez (Anson's captain on his world voyage), desiring to know whether

> "you prest men from the merchant ships under your convoy, when you were near or in the Channel. If not, their lordships desire you to let them know why you did not, the Service being in great want of seamen."

1755. Hawke to Admiralty, from Spithead, October 1, 1755. Explaining his withdrawal from the Blockade of Brest:

> "Most of the men had been pressed, after long voyages, cooped up in tenders and ships at Spithead for many months, and the water in

general long kept in new casks, which occasioned great sickness."
(W. V. Anson, *Life of Lord Anson*, 121.)[1]

1803, April 25 (the renewal of war with France being imminent):

"The officers are not to regard the protection of any description of
persons except those protected pursuant to Acts of Parliament, and
others who by the printed instructions which accompanied the Press
Warrants are forbidden to be impressed, as also such persons as
belong to ships bound to Newfoundland and foreign parts which are
laden and cleared outwards by H.M.'s Customs, the crews of transports
etc. in the service of the Navy and other Boards, ships laden by the
Treasury with provisions for the Armies, and vessels of the Trinity
House."

Rear Admiral [Geo] Campbell to his Captains (*Blockade of Brest*,
1803–05, ed. J. Leyland).

Let us never forget that commerce protection and cruiser patrol-
ling were the wearisome tasks of the Royal Navy; and that the
combination of these with fleet action, never refused, though often
enough with pressed crews miraculously licked into fighting shape,
brought to Britain the command of the sea.

The Press and His Majesty's Customs.

Newcastle.

1756.

March. Mayor of Berwick has in his custody some seamen. The
Regulating Captain is in distress as the Tenders there are full, and
asks Newcastle for the loan of their Bridlington sloop, to convey them.
Newcastle assents.

April. Brown and Sudder, sailors of Newcastle, were impressed on
their arrival.

1764.

June. Adam Sudder, after serving on *H.M.S. Preston* (1756–63)
leaves with a good character from the Captain.

1781. *Re* ship from Memel with timber and raff:

"with respect to the crew it is in vain to thinking of finding them,
they being dispersed in different places and some absconded have
fear of the Press."

---

[1] In 1755 England was at *partial* war with France. "We were seizing their
merchant ships, they were fortifying Dunkirk in defiance of treaties, and before
the end of the year 300 vessels had been taken by our cruisers, and 6000
French seamen carried into our ports. Yet we were not at war!"—Anson,
op. cit., 120.

1782.   Seizure of illicit spirits on the premises of an Innkeeper, who has a House of Rendezvous for the Impress Service.   He had got them from an armed merchantman.

Sunderland.

1778.

"The boys [a gang of five, who had stolen 500 gallons of gin from a warehouse] were tried and the Felony charge proved, but in considera- tion of their very tender age [three being only 11] the Jury brought them in not guilty, and the Court agreed to deliver them to the Impress Service."

Naval Borstal!

Swansea.

1794.   A master attributes the long interval between the day of clearing and the day of discharging his cargo to the Impress.   "Some weeks were lost in Harbour for want of Seamen."

Similarly in January, 1805, the East India Co. complained to the Admiralty that one of their vessels was captured by the enemy because its crew had been so denuded by impressment that it could not put up a decent resistance.

Poole.

1806, July (post-Trafalgar).

A certain Capt. Glynn, employed on Impress Service, having complained "of our refusing to inform him when vessels are released from Quarantine," we observe:

"Our refusal arose from an apprehension that the terror of falling into the hands of the Impress Officer thro' this information of the Customs might induce the Mariners on board to take very opportunity of eluding the vigilance of the Officers of the Cutters, and break from the restraints of Quarantine."
"We have never sanctioned the landing of men from vessels under Quarantine.   All the men (but one), who . . . evaded quarantine, were landed *before* the vessels arrived in Poole Harbour."

To catch the returning mariner, as he came out of quarantine on the Mother Bank (Spithead) was a regular practice and so, when the Press was hot, crews from the Mediterranean, where plague was endemic, often left their ship before she came into port.

His Majesty's Customs and the Quarantine.

Precautions against the introduction of human plague by the performance of quarantine and of cattle disease (distemper) figure

prominently in the Customs Records of 1770–1800. London sets
the pace with stringent warnings. The outports signify compliance
and report on cases that came their way. In 1786 it appears that
Newcastle sent quarantine cases from the Levant to the Humber,

> "this not being a port enumerated in the Order in Council for such a
> service."

In 1789 a Leghorn ship is sheltered till she can go for quarantine to
"White Booth" (wherever that may be, sometimes written "White
Booths").

Mark some of the highlights:—
1770, June 28.

> "A plague stricken ship, the Master and 14 of the crew dead, ejected
> in turn from Malta, Tunis, Naples, and all the Maritine Coast of the
> Republic of Venice."

Watch out for this pariah of the sea!

1770's. Cotton-wool, and textile fabrics, the dreaded carriers of
plague. Ships with such cargoes to perform quarantine, infected
bales to be aired and dried, and hides from proclaimed areas prohibited.

1780. Lurid consular reports from Dalmatia and Greece.

> (1) Pestilential disease at Spalatro, "a city of some note," and
> incidentally the scene of Robert Adam's excavations. "Physicians
> differ. Interest may induce the Venetians to adopt that which is
> most favourable to commercial interest."

> (2) "The Morea is seldom, if ever, quite free from the plague."
> Some Jews are loading currants in a Danish galliot for Jersey or
> Guernsey in small illegal casks for smuggling into England—"the
> greed of gain has no determined limits."

1794. A new peril—Yellow Fever, consequent upon troop move-
ments from the West Indies. Quarantine to be strictly enforced.

Nor was England the only country to take alarm. The century
closes with this in the War Office records: W.O.1.604 (Guernsey
bundle): from Sir Thomas Saumarez (the admiral's brother), staff
officer and inspector of Guernsey militia, to Hew Dalrymple, the Lt.
Govr., Nov., 1800.

> "Express from Paris to Cherbourg, ordering all French privateers
> bringing prizes from England, but particularly from Guernsey or
> Jersey must perform quarantine, 40 days, because English regiments
> had been lately landed in the Islands, who had been employed on the
> Cadiz expedition, and given the plague to the inhabitants."

All this was honey for Malthus (no sham plague, but the good honest Byzantine pest), but it did not come Adam Smith's way. To be sure, he did not like the putrid stinking carcase of a dead dog or cat (I, 74), but that was China's food, not ours; and in summer, with his strawberries, he was safe enough. For when "fruits is in, cats is out." He could speak, therefore, of the calamities of war in terms that the author of the Great Illusion would have found misleadingly mild.

> "In great empires the people who live in the capital, and in the provinces remote from the scene of action, feel, many of them, scarce any inconveniency from the war; but enjoy, at their ease, the amusement of reading in the newspapers the exploits of their own fleets and armies. To them this amusement compensates the small differences between the taxes which they pay on account of the war, and those which they had been accustomed to pay in time of peace. They are commonly dissatisfied with the return of peace, which puts an end to their amusement, and to a thousand visionary hopes of conquest and natural glory, from a longer continuance of the war." (II, 405.)

But, as Sir Roy Harrod points out (*Economic Journal*, September, 1958, p. 537):

> "The British position is probably unique owing to her vast amount of portfolio capital. Her unbroken history of solvency means that she is still carying National Debt representing expenditures in the wars of freedom against Louis XIV, Napoleon, Kaiser William II and Hitler." And may one specify "7 Years War" also?

Chapter VII

COAL (continued)

SWANSEA AND DISTRICT—COAL TRADE AND SMUGGLING—RISE OF
COPPER SMELTING—SEQUENCE OF EXTRACTIVE INDUSTRIES—MODERN
ROLE OF ANTHRACITE—TYNESIDE SHIPPING AND SHIPBUILDING—
CROWLEY'S IRON—GLASS AND TOBACCO BURNING—COASTWISE STONE
—"CARRYING COALS TO NEWCASTLE."

Coal and Secondary Industries

If we mean by Industrial Revolution an economy dominated by
machine power, Adam Smith was pre-industrial revolution. (His
revolution with a capital R, II, 397, was 1688, which incidentally
was Trevelyan's telephone number in the old Cambridge days).
However, as Professor, he had helped to secure a sanctuary for its
principal parent, James Watt, within the walls of Glasgow College—
"deep brooding Watt sitting in his academic shop, studying great
physical powers." So our text at this point will bear the right date,
1776, though it comes in the pages of Boswell's Life of Johnson.
"I sell here, Sir, what all the world desires to have—POWER."
Thus Matthew Boulton, now Watt's partner, to Boswell, when he
was visited by Boswell at Soho, Birmingham. Coal-engendered
power was the *final* triumph of Old King Cole; and therefore in the
eighteenth century Customs Records of Swansea and Newcastle we
must be content to watch the antecedents. One rarely encounters
"machine" or "engine." For Newcastle I noted only two such
mentions.

1755. A warning that the newly patented "machine" for removing ballast may, by slovenly dumping, damage the harbour and
obstruct the exit of "the large colliers by whom our trade is at
present carried on."

1787. "Coal engine" [nature unspecified] from London stopped,
for lack of coast dispatches.

Swansea and District.

The industrialism of Swansea was junior to that of Newcastle,
and less composite; and the evolution is more simple. It is coal,

coal the whole way, outwards, to the South of Ireland and the Channel Islands in chief. In return came *inter alia* alcohol and fats. Ireland had a rich animal husbandry, which favoured the boiling of fats, by the aid of coal, into soap, candles and the like. These products were subject to duties of Excise, and Swansea Customs were kept busy. Adverting in 1750 to "the Act of last session against the Clandestine Importation of such produce," they observed that it was being "slipped in," on limestone boats, carrying limestone coastwise. The master of an Appledore boat, which "generally used the Irish trade," declared to Customs that he had nothing of the sort on board—"come and have a drink." But not all were so polite. In 1763 a master, bound from Waterford to the Isle of Jersey with soap and other goods, and forced to shelter in "Swanzey," abused the Tidesmen who boarded him, removed the soap in defiance of orders, and told the Collector he was "a scrub, a bugbear and a broomstick, and sent to be a plague to him"; whereupon, very properly, the Collector ejected him from the Custom House.

Adam Smith observes that soap was rendered dearer by taxes (I, 80) and regrettably so, because soap was necessary to cleanliness, as were candles to the day's work in long winter nights (II, 358). But there is no reason to suppose that the miners of South Wales worried about cleanliness. Alcohol was a different story. The West Country-men and the Dutchmen came in ballast for their cargoes of coal. The liquor they had on board of course, was only for the ship's crew. But Customs knew better.

In 1769

"a Dutch galliot from Bourdeaux to Amsterdam was stranded in Aberavon Sands in this port. By constant attendance day and night, at the risk of our lives we have secured the whole cargo consisting of 530 h'hds of Burgundy and Claret, which we have lodged in Hon. Mr. Vernon's stables at Briton Ferry, being the only place of safety in that neighbourhood: and have taken every precaution to prevent it being embezzled. The officers behaved with great spirit and resolution by intimidating the country people who were assembled to destroy both ship and cargo."

If one follows the liquor seizures from the 1730's onwards, the sequence roughly is wine and brandy; brandy and gin; then gin, gin, gin, accompanied by bags of tea, with a solitary reference in 1794 to whisky from Cork (spelt without an "e"). But no mention, as yet, of Porson's fancied beverage. (On one occasion, after his host's wine gave out, he forced his way into the lady's apartment and returned in triumph with a bottle of "the best gin he had tasted for a long time," he said after finishing the contents. When Hoppner told his wife that Porson had drunk every drop of her concealed dram, she cried "Drunk every drop of it! My God, it was spirits of wine for the lamp.")

Pitt tried to get to the bottom of it, and called for an enquiry into the amount of illicit spirit imported from August, 1785, to August, 1786; and the price at which it sold. Swansea's reply was illuminating.

> "We think the quantity is considerable from the general use of spirits among the lower ranks of People—about 6000 gallons, which we are informed is sold at the rate of 5, 6 and 7 shillings per gallon, but we cannot state the comparative price, there having been no spirits legally imported here."

If we take the 50 years 1740–90, from the July when Adam Smith matriculated at Oxford to the July when he died, and ask for Great Britain as a whole what proportion duty paid alcohol bore to the total importation, we ask a question to which a precise statistical answer is evidently impossible.

Consider only this from Poole, Mary, 1782:

In transmitting the figures of wine imports at Poole for the last 5 years,

> "we are of opinion that large quantities of wine are run on this coast, particularly by one Isaac Gulliver, a most notorious smuggler, who lives at Kingston [by Corfe Castle] near the sea shore and is professedly a wine merchant, and the better to conceal frauds on the Revenue which he carries on, enters and pays duty for some part of what he imports, and by mixing that with what is run he bids defiance to the officers to seize any wine from him. And they have not at any one instance been able to detect him."

My guess at a percentage figure for the illicit trade over the period is +50 per cent in years of peace and −50 per cent in years of war, when the Press was hot and smugglers were taken into the Navy, or made themselves scarce.

Meanwhile, a second export staple had developed. There was no sort of post-war slump after the Seven Years War. Indeed, the building of a new Customs House was held up (August, 1766) "owing to the increase of shipbuilding at this port." The central feature in the expansion was the growth of copper smelting by the aid of coal—the import of the ore, and the export of the finished product. This was Swansea's speciality, and the lineal ancestor of tin-plate and steel.

A letter of March, 1779, Swansea to London, runs:

"Your Honors. We have received the inclosed copy of a Minute of an application for a drawback on Coals used in smelting copper and lead from mines on the Isle of Anglesea. . . . There are considerable quantities of copper ore imported into this Port from the above Island, which is smelted here with coals which pay no duty. . . . We presume that coals for the purpose of smelting ores may be permitted to be imported into the Isle of Anglesea and the drawback of the duties allowed."

The smelting industry was in Company hands.

October, 1784.

"The English Copper Co. beg leave to represent that they have a Colliery at Margam and Aberavon, which lies in the Bay of Swansea, Glamorgan, from which place it is distant over the Ferry and Sands upwards of 10 miles, and when the Tide is in, the nearest way is then 16 miles. The vessels trading to Margam carry thither copper ore and sometimes a few limestones. They load out with coal and occasionally a loading of copper and metals. The Masters of all these vessels are obliged to go to Swansea for a Cocket and Clearance, by which means (besides the Journey) they often lose the opportunity of sailing upon a Spring Tide and are detained in consequence a fortnight."

They ask for the removal of this delay.

Signed "by command of the English Copper Coy.
                                            G. Smith Secry."

February, 1785.

"There are no ships in the Foreign Trade using the Harbour of Neath in which any foreign goods are imported, the trade to that Port is mostly in the Coasting Business, and the imports are chiefly copper ore from Cornwall and merchandize from other ports in England. The exports from thence are coal and copper, which are carried coastwise to Ireland, Man and the Islands of Guernsey and Jersey."

January, 1788. Certain Copper and Lead Smelting Companies and others plea for the unification of the services on either side of the River of Burry, each [sc. Llanelly Customs and Swansea Customs] considers only its own takings, and this is undesirable in view of increasing trade.

Swansea has no objection to *barges* using either side, but there is danger to the Revenue if *ships* may do so. (Lead apparently was a "newcomer," for in sending to London, 1786, a sample of the ore, 2s. 6d. carriage paid, they asked London "What is lead?")

South Wales was emerging rapidly from its rural past; yet the County of Glamorgan was still a great grower of wool, and the limestone from the Hon. Lord Vernon's Manor at Briton Ferry employed as many as eight ships. But it was the new metallurgy which puzzled the Customs:

> "It was not copperas but a transmuted metallic substance denominated by the traders 'snuff ore,'"

they were told in 1797. And in 1799:

> "We do not find the Orders in Council prohibit the export from this Port of Copper in Cakes Tiles or Boxes etc., if not in sheets Bolts, Nails etc. applicable to Naval purposes."

But by Mr. Fawkener's order, *via* Mr. [Deacon] Hume, of 1794, flat Bottoms for Kettles, Plates for Sides thereof and for Braziers were permitted.

In Swansea, as in the smelting industries elsewhere, the rule observed by Stanley Jevons in general held good—the lighter ore to the heavier fuel; and Dorset clay was to behave in somewhat similar wise. After 1815, when the disbanding of the armies caused a sharp decline in the demand for salted fish, the exploitation of the Corfe-Wareham clays adjoining Poole took its place. Hand-dug, taken in farm carts to an inlet, and then in 50-ton barges to Poole, it was carried thence to Liverpool, to the amount of 20,000 tons and more per annum, in brigs and brigantines formerly in the Newfoundland trade. By 1840 (it was said) nearly one-third of English pottery was fashioned from Poole clay.

But local works continued to produce bricks, pipes and tiles. (The references to *pipe* clay in eighteenth century records I take to refer to clay pipes for tobacco smoking.) And in the present century, 1920–30, Italian schooners carried Dorset clay to Italian ports—Savona, Civita Vecchia, Leghorn; reminding one of the lowly end of the Nova Scotian windjammers as carriers of guano from the Chinchas of Peru. Guano was the excrement of sea-fowls, gathered from the rainless islands along that Coast. Graham and Peel used it and sang its praises to one another; inside three years (1852–54) one Liverpool firm alone sold over £5 million worth of it, as Tooke tells us in his *History of Prices*. The sequence of the extractive industries—of fish and fertilisers, stones and clays, coal and the

metals, petroleum and natural gas, how cardinal and yet how difficult to fit into the pattern of foreign and domestic trade!

But Jevons' rule was not a universal. In our day the steel works
and Scottish steel workers came to the new ore field of Corby,
Northants, because the ore there was rich and fuel was available from
Midland coalfields over a developed railway system. And it has
worked out to the great and deserved advantage of the Kettering
Industrial Cooperative Society.

The lure of history is the way it runs out into the present; and,
being particularly interested in Canada and the Channel Islands, I
allow myself these quotations from *The Anthracite Coal Industry of
the Swansea District* by A. E. C. Hare, University College of Swansea,
Pamphlet No. 5.

Canada.

"Before 1914 the export market for Welsh Anthracite was mainly
confined to Europe. . . . The war brought about considerable
changes. . . . First of these [new markets] in importance is Canada,
which has developed from very small beginnings to be one of the chief
outlets."

"The domestic consumer in Canada favours anthracite almost
exclusively and the stoves are constructed for the purpose of burning
that fuel."

"The import of Welsh Anthracite into Canada was greatly assisted
by the very low freights prevailing. . . . The cost of taking anthracite from Swansea to Quebec or Montreal, a distance of about 2,800
or 2,900 miles respectively, has been only about 2s. a ton more than
the cost of shipping anthracite from Swansea to London."

Channel Islands.

"The Channel Islands have developed an extensive industry supplying
the English market with vegetables [Guernsey appears to specialise
in tomatoes for Belfast; and in the summer, I have been told, the
tomato boats bring over a passenger or two], and the demand for
anthracite has developed *pari passu* with the growth of this trade
The Channel Islands are peculiar in that they take over 90 per cent of
their imports in large unbroken anthracite, which is used in this state
for heating greenhouses, for which purpose its slow burning qualities
make it particularly suitable." Wandering round Guernsey one
sees the hard shiny lumps beside the furnaces serving the ubiquitous
glass houses on the Island.

Tyneside.

As an economic unit Tyneside stretched northwards along the
coast as far as Blythe and upstream beyond Newcastle for some

6 miles. On the north bank was North Shields—Tynemouth; on
the South, South Shields, which lay within the ambit of Sunderland.

The industrialism of Tyneside was senior to that of Swansea and
district, and more composite. There was no single secondary
industry as outstanding as that of copper smelting in Swansea.
But it all rested from first to last on coal; and today the Tyne, in
association with the adjacent river systems of the Wear and Tees,
forms a complex whole, which, like the Clyde, has flourished on
shipping, shipbuilding and marine engineering, with the Merchant
Marine and the Royal Navy as joint customers. Clydeside, Tyneside and the Durham Coast owed their shipbuilding to their
proximity to coal and iron fields. Belfast had to import these
materials, but possessed a sheltered water, with no lack of strong and
competent labour, so that the Lagan became the shipyard of the
Mersey, which could not, except on the Birkenhead side, afford the
space for shipbuilding. But in the eighteenth century, as seen
through the spectacles of the Customs, the industrialism of Tyneside
was patchy, and rather incidental, so dominating was the coal trade
to London.

We have figures for Newcastle shipping, e.g. 1789–89, from the
Register of Shipping under the Act of 1786.

Local builders: 41 ships from 21 yards; leading builder Ed. Murphy
(Mosley & Co.) at Howden Pans, with 5. Place where most ships
were built, South Shields.

Ships on Register.

British built	423
British Plantation built	49
Foreign built	16
Largest tonnage group	201–250 tons

Leading types, number of, brigantines (217), barques (101).

As I give these figures I have in mind the sight from Sunderland,
July, 1958, of a huge oil tanker on the stocks at Monk Wearmouth,
on the north side of the river Wear, and others of like dimension
just beyond.   It reminded me of Harland and Wolff's, as one enters
Belfast Harbour.

1725. Blyth Nook is become a place of great trade both for
coasting and oversea vessels.

1736.   Arrival of iron by "Mr. Crowley's manufacture at Swalwell [*Swallow-spring*, up the Tyne on the Durham side, 5 miles west of Newcastle]."[1]

"As to Iron and all other weighable merchandise imported from or exported to ports beyond seas (lead excepted), the King's Scales only are made use of."

1737.   A ship comes to Newcastle to load coal and grind stones.

1743.   Procedure for ships outwards bound with "coals, grindstones or salt [the salt boiled on the salt pans]."

1744.   Mr. Crowley's iron ware from Swalwell is crowding out the coals.—(One walks today from Blaydon past Scotswood Bridge and then along the tow path and over a footbridge to the junction of the Tyne with the Derwent, which is here spanned by a wide bridge carrying rail and motor traffic.   Touching the Tyne is Raine & Co. Delta Iron & Steel Works, marked PRIVATE; so one bears right, past more iron works, to the village of Swalwell, half a mile inland. The bus station adjoins the graceful war memorial: over a 100 fallen (1914–18) from this one mining village—N.F. (Northumberland Fusiliers), D.L.I. (Durham Light Infantry) and Royal Naval Division.)

1750.   References to "British Plantation Pig Iron."

1756.   Proprietors of Glass Houses and the disposal of Tobacco Ashes—already an old story, which crops up again and again.

Thus in 1733, Customs say *re* damaged tobacco,

"we have formerly applied to the proprietors of a Glass House—to burn it there.   But thus burnt the ashes will fetch nothing, and the smell is so offensive that the Glass Works refuse further leave."

---

[1] Swalwell adjoins Winlaton and Blaydon, and the Official Guide to Blaydon reads, p. 20, "The abundance of coal at Winlaton was one of the reasons which induced Ambrose Crowley, the London ironmonger, to establish his factory there in 1690, when he was forced to leave Sunderland because the foreign workmen were subjected to persecution.   Workmen were brought from the Continent and from London to the factory, which later was extended to Swalwell and Winlaton Mill," where most of the heavy work was done. "Rules for the care of tools and the good government of the factory, laid down by Crowley and his son, are contained in the Winlaton Law Book now in the British Museum."—Add. 34,555.   "Law Book of the Crowley Iron Works, Winlaton: a lined folio of 381 pages, with Table of Contents and Index; prefaced by 2 letters of 1702 from Crowley at Winlaton to Sir William Bowes, Bart., House of Commons, Westminster.

And similarly in 1756:

Glass House Proprietor will take condemned tobacco to his house and burn it, in return for the ashes.

> "He won't lend it for the purpose, but we are to look upon it as a favour that he will permit it to be burn there."

Newcastle advises acceptance—ashes fetch only 3d. a bushel—and London reluctantly accepts. In later entries the usual statement is "Glass houses will burn tobacco for the ashes."   ,
But it is to the Liverpool of the 1770's that we must turn to understand what tobacco burning meant. (To Bristol we cannot turn because the Reform Bill rioters burnt their Customs records.) A Petition thence of 1777 reads:

> "Our lands and houses must sink in value. The furniture of our houses is spoiled, life is rendered comfortless to all, and many are afflicted with sore eyes."

But no mention of lung cancer; nor, on the other hand, of its place in Sir William Temple's programme of plague-prevention:

> "burnt Burgomo pitch, and made as many servants as they could, after ye smoke was gone, take tobacco a great part of the day."

1756. Lead
> "is shipped for exportation from Blaydon at a Quay belonging to Sr Walter Blackett about 4 miles from Newcastle. The piles of pig are weighed and put on board keels."

Lead weights tested frequently.

1766. Case of a British-built ship from Carolina lengthened in a foreign port, Hamburg:
> "to the discouragement of the Trade of Ship-building in these Kingdoms, and to the decrease of H.M.'s Revenue by the use of foreign materials."

1771. Report on additional Quays:
In addition to the "legal quays," there are "indulgencies" to other places, both for imports and exports. For exports—salt pans at Shields etc.; lead at Blaydon and "Mr. Bowes staith"; copperas at three works on the Tyne; glass at Seaton Sluice; coal on all parts of the Tyne from Newcastle to Shields—"of practice imemorial." Discretion rests with the Collector.

1783. An entry to remind that there was more than coal outwards and timber inwards. Seized, for an irregularity, from two Algerine ships:

"Red morocco skins, duly stamped by Customs: 107 pairs of slippers: and sixpounds and tenpence in copper half-pence." Slippers returned "by way of compassion": half-pence "base, but may have been received in the way of trade."

1790. An apprentice of Faversham, Kent, going ashore to choose three crates of earthenware, missed his boat. Customs seized his ware "from lack of a coasting sufferance!"

1790–92. Lists of Grindstones and Flagstones outwards; Slates, Paving stones, Fire stones inwards (as per table).

1794. Limestones carried coastwise from the Rocks on the Northumberland coast are dumped at convenient spots to be collected "at their leisure" by farmers for manure. By the Stone Act limestones are exempt from duty, if accompanied by *dispatches*. Shippers say this holds up the carriage and hurts farming—they therefore ask for a simple *certificate* instead.

This is in line with a Memorial of 1768 to Sunderland by the shippers of limestone and burnt lime from the Wear to Northumberland, Durham and Yorkshire for use on the strong clay soils there. They have been in the business over 60 years. They work the stone all winter, in preparation for the summer trade. Sunderland now demands dispatches, though hitherto there has been neither application to nor suffrance from the Customs. The profit is only 6d. per chaldron for lime, 8d. per ton for stone. The cost and delay will cause the trade to be totally laid off, unless the farmer pays double; and this will distress an extensive corn country, lay idle a number of labourers or sailors employed in this business, and will not improve the revenue. A vigorous and well-phrased plea.

In Tobacco we had the pleasure of introducing Mr. and Mrs. Simm of dubious morality. In Coal we meet, April, 1799, a more conformable gentleman in the person of Richard Fairbairn of Newcastle, nominated to be a boatman at this port, who has not yet abjured the Roman Catholic religion, sometimes goes to that chapel and sometimes to the Established Church, but intends to qualify according to law—"wery pleasant and conformable," as Mr. Weller senior said of mannerly Mary.

It might seem impossible to end this Chapter more happily than

by a final quotation from the *Wealth of Nations*.   Yet this is not so.
The palm goes to *Tom Jones*, Book 8, Chapter 4:

> "Sure sir," answered the Barber [when battered Tom talked of enlisting], "you are too wise to carry a broken head thither; for that would be carrying coals to Newcastle."

Tom Jones is 1749; and in February, 1743, it had actually happened, to the bewilderment of Newcastle Customs, who did not know whether to charge by Newcastle or Winchester measure, till London decided for Winchester.   The case had arisen thus.   A Sunderland master, on the point of clearing with coals, received a profitable order for lead to Havre de Grace.   Therefore he unloaded his coal at Newcastle, took in lead there, and sailed away for France.   And so it goes, contrariwise, in this quaint world of ours.   Headstrong Tom survived all dangers and gained at the end the adorable Sophia; while patient Adam, for all his philosophy, could never bring himself to put the question to his "maid of Fife."

The *Wealth of Nations* is great stuff, but common honesty compels us to admit that nothing in Adam Smith or Fielding or Dickens matches Newcastle Customs at their best.   For here is life, real and entire.   Listen to the Petition of William Tynemouth of South Shields at present (November, 1805) confined in Durham gaol for smuggling.   Your Petitioner hath a dear wife, five children and an aged mother, all chargeable to the Township of South Shields. He asks for liberty and the return of something not less precious: to wit, a Vestal Virgin, made of plaster of Paris, bronzed over and intended as a staircase lamp for a present to his Aunt Mrs. Renwick: value £7 10s. 0d.   It was shipped aboard the *Minerva* bound for Newcastle, but lacking a coastal dispatch was seized by Customs. Minerva; Vestal Virgin; the staircase lamp that leads aloft; the final outrage.   Surely their Honors would not suffer sacrilege such as this; and not only sacrilege, but the possible addition of a penny to the Poor's rate of South Shields.

AFTER-THOUGHT

John Logan [a minister of the Scottish Church] to Adam Smith.

London, August 20, '87.

Dear Sir, . . .

Lord George Gordon has returned to London and what is more extraordinary has become a Jew. He lodges at the house of my Taylor, goes to the synagogue on Saturdays and eats no meat but what is killed by the Jews. He is said to be making love to a rich Jewess, but I expect his plans are deeper and that he intends to set up as Messiah, a trade which has never been very successful. He set up a hideous and horrid roar when he was circumcised. (W. R. Scott, *Adam Smith as Student and Professor*, 305.)

"Science is the great antidote to the poison of enthusiasm and superstition." (*Wealth of Nations*, II, 281.)

When I first went to York to see my grandfather's chain brake in the Railway Museum there, railways appealed to young and old alike. But now they are rather passé. The interest of today is in Crime Stories and the Polar Route. Yet the glamour of the Tyburn jig lives on, rare though hangings now are and long since closed to public view.

Once only has the sovereignty of hangman Dennis been seriously challenged, namely by Conan Doyle in the Los Amigos Fiasco. But there is a flaw in that tale. For after they had failed to electrocute their man, failed to hang him, and failed to shoot him, they might have called in Dr. Guillotin, and not even the creator of Sherlock Holmes could have persuaded us that the body of Duncan Warner would run about for hundreds of years, unaccompanied by a head.

I was often, in *Barnaby Rudge*, to Tyburn (they hanged Hugh's mother there) in the company of Mr. Dennis, and I regret Adam Smith's slur on his meritorious profession:

"the most detestable of all employments, that of public executioner,"
I, 102;

for whereas athletes merely "work out," helpful Dennis "worked off" all who came his way)—so often, indeed, that I never guessed that York had a Tyburn and that it was at York Dick Turpin was hanged.

The end of Brock's "Alfred" we know well. He fell in action on Queenston Heights, Niagara, with Macdonnell, Brock's aide-de-camp, on his back. (Brock had dismounted and advanced on foot up-hill, McDonnell rode past on "Alfred" and all three met their death that day—October 13, 1812.) But the end of Black Bess is lost to legend; yet the fame of Dick Turpin had been something less, "if he'd ne'er rode to York on his bonnie Black Bess."

Of Dick Turpin's own end, since the publication of *Immortal Turpin* by Arty Ash and Julius E. Day we now know what there is to know (and, perhaps, a little more).

"Arriving at the fatal spot he talked some time to the hangman, and presented him with a small Ivory Whistle. He then mounted the ladder, and feeling his right leg tremble, he stamped it impatiently down with an air of assumed courage, as though he were afraid of discovering any signs of fear"—And without waiting for the cart to be drawn away, he flung himself from the ladder and expired instantly.

And the body? *Ipswich Journal*, Saturday, April 21, 1739:

"They write from York that an attempt was made by the surgeons of that Place to have got the Body of Dick Turpin, but the Mob, having heard that it was dug up, and being informed where it was, went and rescued it and reinterred it, having strewn it over with Lime to prevent it being anatomised."

His grave is in St. George's Churchyard, George Street, Fishergate, York.

So today, in addition to York Minster, we must visit in York Castle "Pompey's Parlour," the cell for condemned prisoners, in which he lay; and see in the Yorkshire Museum the chains which bound him. And if we are document-minded, we shall try to locate this in "Records of York Castle."

"A meeting was held at the Castle of York on March 1, 1739. It was decided to build a gallows on (or opposite to) Knavesmire, the present racecourse, which, after its namesake in London, should be called the Tyburn of York. It was also resolved that Master Joseph Penny, Joiner, of Blocke Street in the City of York, do build the said gallows forthwith at the cost of £10 15s. 0d., and these new gallows were completed by the 7th of March."

Sceptics there may be still, but at least they cannot challenge the Baptismal Entry of Richardus Turpin in the Parish Register of Hempstead, Essex.

Pace the Master, Science, when it lacks a counter-poise to itself, creates the spiritual vacuum which Romance and Superstition are quick to fill.

When bishops had become great barons,

> "the inferior ranks of people . . . were provoked by the vanity, luxury, and expence of the richer clergy, who appeared to spend on their own pleasures, what had always been regarded as the patrimony of the poor." (*Wealth of Nations*, II, 288.)

How different Dick Turpin! Once (the tradition runs), when he had robbed a poor woman on her way back from market, and she told him if he took the money she would be in distress for rent, he found out where she lived and threw into the window through the glass Gold and Silver to the amount of six pounds.

But no mercy for episcopal informers:

> Says Turpin "You shall eat your words,
> With a sarse of leaden bul-let";
> So he puts a pistol to his mouth,
> And he fires it down his gul-let.

Thanks be to gunpowder. For, as our Bible tells us (II, 202):

> "The invention of fire-arms, an invention which at first sight appears to be so pernicious, is certainly favourable both to the permanency and to the extension of civilisation."

Hail Columbia! A Charter, belike, for your Atom Bomb—"for making war upon the universal airth," as prescribed by Elijah Pogram.

W. R. Scott closes his very well informed treatise with an Appendix VII on "Adam Smith and his Russian admirers of the eighteenth century" by a Professor of Leningrad. I wonder if they or their successors of today ever got to this on II, 283, Book V, Chapter II, Part 2, Article 3*d*:

> "Fear is in almost all cases a wretched instrument of government, and ought in particular never to be employed against any order of men who have the smallest pretensions to independency."

INDEX

c = **Chapter**